Lessons Learned From My Father

Lori Campbell M.D.

Mom and Dad (1953)

Mom and Dad (2008)

To Mom

Thank you for encouraging me to write about the love of your life.

How blessed I've been to know the comfort of your tiny hands.

I thank God for you.

Keep flying; he's still watching over you.

I love you more than words can say.

"And let us consider how we may spur one another on toward love and good deeds."

Hebrews 10:24

TABLE OF CONTENTS

Boat on the Sea of Galilee

Sunrise over the Sea of Galilee

PREFACE

In the spring of 2008, I had the privilege of traveling to Israel with a group of individuals from two churches. My husband, Bill, and I decided to celebrate our 25th wedding anniversary by taking this trip. From my teen years on, I had always wanted to sail on the Sea of Galilee, for reasons I cannot explain. As I aged and my faith grew, I pictured all of the things Christ said and did around this body of water. I was thrilled to finally have the chance to see and touch the very land and water I had read so much about.

While in Tiberias, we stayed at a hotel which was on the shores of the Sea of Galilee. We spent several days touring the area, marveling each morning at the beautiful sunrises. We did sail on the Sea of Galilee, but it wasn't what I had anticipated. I had always pictured myself alone in a boat, quietly sailing on this famous body of water. Instead, approximately 50 people were on the boat, singing and dancing as we traveled from one side of the Sea to the other. Everyone was smiling and laughing, except me. I wanted to be alone. My spirit longed to reflect on Christ's teachings and travels, on the very water He touched.

As I fell asleep our last night in Tiberias, I was sad thinking about leaving this incredible place. This was the area where Jesus had gathered His disciples, walked on water, calmed the storm, performed many miracles, and reappeared to His disciples after His resurrection.

At 4 am, I awoke crying. I heard a voice say, "Arise and go to the water's edge." Without hesitation, I dressed and walked to the shore. Many catfish were swimming in the shallow waters near the beach, a cat was taking an early morning stroll, and birds were already singing praises.

Tears streamed down my face as I prayed for many individuals and sang the song, *You Are Holy*, by Michael W. Smith. When I sang, "You're the Great I AM," I knew I was in His presence.

I heard the words: "I know you by name. You are mine. Your walk is between you and me; give all of yourself. You don't need a symbol to remind you of me. I am inside of you---I AM." It was then the surrounding hills seemed to be echoing, "I AM."

I was not afraid. I felt blessed that God was so compassionate to meet me alone, by the waters I had longed to see and touch because of Him. I had never referred to God as "I AM," except in song, but knew that God called himself "I AM," as recorded in Exodus 3:13-15 and that Yahweh is derived from the Hebrew word for I AM.

God continued to speak to me and impressed upon me that I was not to dwell on earthly things. I was told I had nothing to fear, that I should be gentle and kind, and should not compare myself to others.

Not wanting to forget any of His words, I ran back to my hotel room and retrieved my journal and Bible. I quickly recorded everything that had occurred. Suddenly, it was as if someone was controlling my right hand as I penned the following words in less than two minutes.

Galilee…my beloved Galilee

standing at the water's edge

I hear the words

proclaiming from the hills,

I AM.

Do not doubt…do not fear…

for **I AM** always near.

I will catch you…I will break your fall,

give me not a part…

GIVE ME ALL.

I know your name,

for you are mine.

Keep me close,

> for **I AM** thine.

I AM

In my darkest of days,

> let me never forget this praise.

I am sealed by the blood of the lamb.

I hear Him calling,

I AM, I AM!

JUBILATION

> fills my heart.

Oh Galilee, we will never part.

Having read scripture, but not knowing where to find a particular verse, I felt compelled to turn to Matthew 14:31 which says:

Immediately Jesus reached out his hand and caught him. "You of little faith," he said, "why did you doubt?"

I then turned to Matthew 28:20

"… and teaching them to obey everything I have commanded you. And surely I am with you always, to the very end of the age."

I believe God led me to these verses to share His message. He wants to wipe away our fears and doubts. Peter had the courage to step out of the boat on the Sea of Galilee, but when the wind came up, he panicked. He took his eyes off of Jesus and began to sink. We don't need to try to walk on water to start sinking. When we doubt the existence or power of Jesus, we sink in our own ignorance. God wants to assure us that "Jesus Christ is the same yesterday, today, and forever" (Hebrews 13:8). God will never leave us or forsake us.

As we taxied in the airplane on a Tel Aviv runway, during our last minutes in Israel, I heard God say, "Write your story and write mine as well." I remember thinking, "I have no idea what that means."

Months later, I began to write down various memories, so as to preserve them for future generations. The trip to Israel had reminded me that without a written record, so much history is lost. The more I wrote, the more I realized the valuable lessons my father had taught me. Through his words and actions he modeled scriptural teachings. It was that realization which led to this book. My father's lessons have enabled me to tell my story and God's as well, because God's lessons were my father's lessons.

I feel so fortunate to have been raised by a man who was an exceptional role model in all aspects of his life. The greatest blessing is to have had an earthly father who enabled me to grasp the love of my Heavenly Father.

Whether you are in the midst of parenting your own child or reflecting back on your own childhood as you read these stories, I hope you will enjoy and possibly learn from them. Although there are many individuals who did not have the love of an earthly father, I want to assure them that there is a Father whose love is available to anyone who desires to know Him. If you seek Him, you will find Him. The Lord never forsakes those who seek Him (Psalm 9:10).

It is my prayer that all men strive to be fathers who reflect the love of the Lord. That kind of love has a ripple effect down through generations, which enables family members to understand the love of our Heavenly Father. I hold near and dear the lessons learned from my earthly father and my Heavenly Father, and I hope you will, too.

Dad on high school tumbling squad

Dad in Air Force uniform (1953)

INTRODUCTION

My father was born in 1932. As the first child, he was named after his father, who worked as a truck driver. Dad inherited his good looks, curly blond hair and baby blue eyes.

Dad worked at the local theater and carried cement blocks for his uncles as a teen. It was the latter job that provided him with arms like the cartoon character Popeye. His physical strength enabled him to be active on the tumbling squad in high school.

After graduation, Dad worked at the local paper mill until serving in the Korean War. He specialized in propeller operation serving duty stateside in Kansas and California.

Dad married his high school love, my mother, Suzanne, in 1954. After his military duty, he attended college on the GI Bill while working nights to support his wife and two daughters. He was the only member of his immediate family to graduate with an advanced degree, with majors in physics and mathematics and a minor in geology.

Teaching was my father's forte. His early career was spent in high-school settings where he also coached tennis, swimming, and golf. During this time, he was blessed with his third child, a son. While working and during the summer months, Dad earned his master's degree. When my older sister reached her teens, my father took a teaching position at the local vocational school. His specialty was hydraulics (fluid power), training many who would later accept jobs across the country. After over 30 years of teaching thousands of students, he retired.

Although Dad officially retired from the field of education, he never stopped teaching. His words and actions taught lessons that few others are able to teach.

My father illustrated that one person can make a difference. His lessons will go on though his books remain closed.

SEEK AND YOU WILL FIND

Matthew 7:7

"Ask and it will be given to you, seek and you will find; knock and the door will be opened to you."

SEEK AND YOU WILL FIND

I became a treasure hunter at the age of four. Growing up, one of our frequent family outings was rock hunting, in particular, agate hunting. Agates are a type of quartz with distinctive, varied-color banding that makes them quite beautiful. I remember finding my first large agate while throwing a temper tantrum atop a rock pile in a gravel pit. It was a hot summer day and my preschool patience had expired. I wanted to return to our car and head for home. My dad, being the Indiana Jones type, did not agree. His motto seemed to be that if you looked long enough and hard enough, you would eventually find what you were seeking. Sweaty and angry, I began to throw rock after rock from my seated position. I enjoyed hearing the noise as each one met its new destination. After multiple tosses, I picked up an egg-sized stone, which glistened as the sunlight hit its surface. Wiping away my sweat and tears, I screamed, "Dad, come here!" He quickly approached me and I excitedly rose to my feet and scurried down the rock pile. "Look," I exclaimed, as I held out my newly found treasure for him to inspect. A wide grin spread across his face. "It's a beauty, Lor," he said. I will never forget that feeling of excitement and achievement.

We spent hours in gravel pits and always left with "treasures." My father usually seemed to have the largest and most beautiful "finds." On that particular day, however, I had found the Holy Grail. From that day forward, my father's positive attitude of discovery would be embedded in my mind and spirit.

Perhaps my learned passion has even bordered on obsession as I've aged. Wherever I am, I'm always looking for a "treasure." Believe it or not, this treasure is most often a rock---and I don't mean a diamond. Dad studied geology at the college level, so I was fortunate to learn a lot about minerals and rocks from him. Entities such as geodes, mica, hematite, and cinnabar gave me an appreciation for natural "treasures." My daughters have confessed embarrassment by my joy in spotting an agate in the landscaping river rock at various restaurants and businesses. Not only do I spot them, but I've been known to jump out of the car while waiting for fast food in order to retrieve them.

Agates bring me joy thanks to my treasure-hunting memories. They remind me of my dad---of home---of simpler times. They reinforce my passion of discovery.

Several years ago, when I was having health problems, my parents came to my home to visit and cheer me up. When it was time for them to leave, I ventured outside to see them off. No sooner had their car disappeared when I looked down at some ground roses and noticed a large agate in the stones surrounding these plants. Convinced that my father had intentionally planted it there for me to find, I smiled. Hours later I phoned home to thank him for the "gift." "Lor, I swear I don't know what you are talking about," was his response. Perhaps it was God's gift to me that day. Either way, it truly brought a smile to my face and a much-needed boost to my spirit.

Lesson Learned:

My father taught that there was a thrill in seeking as well as in finding. Seeking teaches perseverance and instills fortitude. It is only by seeking that agates, answers, and God are found. May we all remember to enjoy the journey as we seek each and every treasure.

KEEP YOUR EYES AND EARS OPEN

Proverbs 20:12

"Ears that hear and eyes that see, the Lord has made them both."

KEEP YOUR EYES AND EARS OPEN

When I was five my father was working toward his master's degree during the summer months at Ole Miss in Oxford, Mississippi. Our family lived in a dormitory called Guess Hall and we ate our meals at the campus cafeteria. My parents thought it best to enroll my sister, Jill, and me in swimming lessons and summer school art courses to keep us busy and out of the dorm. Most of the children in these activities lived in the residential community and had no campus affiliation.

One particular day, my art teacher announced that each student was to bring an empty mustard jar to class the next day. My heart raced upon hearing those words. Shortly thereafter, my father appeared at the classroom door, ready to drive my sister and me "home." Upon reaching our car, he noticed my unusual quietness. With a concerned look he asked, "Is something wrong, Lor?" Trying to hold back tears, I quietly replied, "There's nothing you can do to help me, Dad." He tenderly reached for my hand and said, "Let me at least try." Tears started to stream down my cheeks. I looked up into his empathetic blue eyes and stated, "I need an empty mustard jar for art class tomorrow. I know we don't have one, and the cafeteria only has those small mustard packets." "Oh, that is a problem now, isn't it?" was his response. I couldn't understand the grin that came over his face as we left the parking lot. I felt better having at least been able to share my dilemma, but I didn't know why Dad looked so relieved. Shortly thereafter, he stopped at a small grocery mart and left the car. Minutes later, he returned with a small brown paper bag clutched in his left hand. I was shocked as he handed the bag to me and told me to look inside. I suspected a treat awaited me, thinking Dad was trying in his usual way to bolster my spirits. To my surprise and horror, a small jar of French's yellow mustard stared back at me as I peered in. My heart raced again. Arriving at the dorm, Dad looked my way. "What's wrong, Lori? Didn't you say you needed a mustard jar for class tomorrow?" I nodded. I didn't understand how he had not heard the word, *empty*. "Oh dad, you don't get it!" I shrieked. "It has to be empty! You are the only one in the family who eats mustard, and even you can't eat a whole jar in one night!" I could tell he was trying not to smile as we exited the car. We climbed the stairs to our dorm rooms in silence.

As he opened the door to the main room, he called out a loud hello to my mother and younger brother, Scott. I followed my dad in, clutching the small brown bag in my hand. "Did you pick something up at the store?" Mom asked. I couldn't say a word. "Yup," Dad replied as he reached for the bag. "Lori needs a mustard jar for class tomorrow, so I stopped and picked one up." Dad then opened the sack and showed my mom the jar. "Lor's worried because the jar needs to be empty, and she knows I can't eat all of this in one night." Mom and Dad exchanged glances before he twisted the lid, walked to the small sink in the room, and dumped all of the mustard down the drain. He rinsed the jar until it was spotless and then handed it to me, grinning ear to ear. I smiled too, not just because I had the empty mustard jar I needed, but because I had the smartest dad in the world.

It's been forty-five years since my father handed me that jar. The next day it was filled with marbles and water to be used as a paperweight, but I prefer to remember it being empty.

Lesson Learned:

My father was perceptive. He was observant and noticed the little things. He was never afraid to act if he sensed something was wrong or someone needed help. Listening and observing gives us the information we need to lift burdens, regardless of size.

REALIZE NO MAN KNOWS ALL

1 Corinthians 13:12

"Now we see but a poor reflection as in a mirror; then we shall see face to face. Now I know in part; then I shall know fully, even as I am fully known."

REALIZE NO MAN KNOWS ALL

There were three deaths in my family during my early childhood years. The two that had the greatest emotional impact were the loss of my maternal grandfather and a paternal aunt. Both of these losses occurred when I was around the age of 5.

Because I'd been taken to Sunday school on a regular basis, I knew something about heaven, though I'd never thought much about it until confronted with the sudden absence of relatives who had been part of my everyday life. After their burials, I was plagued with many questions and fears regarding death and heaven. It seemed my fears were the worst at night as I dreaded waking up to find another member of the family gone. I couldn't understand that if heaven was an actual place, why couldn't we go and visit?

I decided to talk to the smartest man I knew---my dad. The timing was perfect, as he was working outside building a two-car garage on our property. I opted to sit at the base of his ladder and ask the questions for which I had no answers.

I looked up, somewhat blinded by the sunlight, and asked, "Dad, where do we really go when we die?"

He paused for a moment and then replied, "We hope to go to heaven."

"Well, where exactly is heaven?" I asked.

"Only God really knows," was his response.

"What's it like there, Dad?"

He pounded in a couple of nails before he looked down and said, "It's a wonderful place, Lori."

"How do you know that, Dad?"

"The Bible tells us so," he answered.

"What do we do there?" was the next question.

"I'm not sure, Lori."

How could he not be sure, I wondered. "Do you think you or Mom will be going there soon?"

My father's unexpected response stopped my line of inquisition. "There are some things, Lori, we just don't know," was his final answer.

I was speechless. Dad knew everything. He'd always known the answer to any question I'd ever asked. Right before my eyes, he was tumbling off the pedestal he had always been on. It was a shock to find out he wasn't all-knowing.

I walked away bewildered and disappointed as my father continued to pound nails in an almost rhythmic fashion. It would take years for me to realize that it was my father's honesty which kept him from being my idol that day.

Lesson Learned:

Death and separation are hard concepts to grasp at any age. My dad, like any parent, probably wanted to assure me that he would always be there for me. Sadly, a parent can't do that. The truth is simply that none of us are guaranteed our next breath. My father did not pretend to be God that day or any day. As humans we won't always have the answers. As devastating as it was for me to realize at such a young age that my father didn't know everything, his honesty helped me to later realize that no human is "pedestal worthy."

DISCIPLINE WITH LOVE

Proverbs 29:17

"Discipline your son, and he will give you peace; he will bring delight to your soul."

DISCIPLINE WITH LOVE

In my early elementary school years, it often seemed I was deemed responsible for every sibling altercation in our family. Though I was the middle child, I was just as big as my older sister Jill. I was four years older than my baby brother, so he was never even considered to be at fault, and Jill, who was three years older, seemed to know just what to say to escape punishment. I talked too, but typically in an argumentative fashion. Instead of apologizing or accepting my punishment (which usually entailed standing in a corner of the living room or hallway), I would debate with my father regarding his "ruling." I demanded to tell my side of the story and *always* had to have the last word. Because of my verbal rhetoric, I have the distinct honor of being the only one of his children he spanked.

After one such spanking, I decided that since my "last word" did not work, I would have the "last action." After my father spanked me with an open hand across my clothed buttocks, I dramatically fell to the floor, eyes closed, tongue hanging out to the side of my mouth. My father was a hunter, so I'd seen numerous dead deer hanging in our garage during many hunting seasons. At this point in time, I felt so smart knowing what a *dead body* looked like. Surely, my father would think that he had killed me, and then he'd feel sorry that he didn't let me have my way!

I was shocked that my appearance did not arouse some level of concern from my dad or my mom. I would intermittently open my eyes ever so slightly to see if anyone had noticed what a terrible state I was in. After what seemed like hours, I heard footsteps approach and braced myself for a scream. Not one noise was made when my mother "resurrected" me by pouring a small glass of water on my face. Little did I know that it was my tongue, which had betrayed me---again!

Lesson Learned:

As a child I, like so many children, needed to be reminded that I was not an adult. It was disrespectful for me to argue with my father, and he was right not to tolerate that behavior. This story is not about advocating physical discipline but rather not tolerating disrespect. Too many parents allow young children to behave in ways that are disrespectful; these behaviors then become habitual. It is a parent's job to step in with love, discipline, and consistency. I am grateful for a father who did just that.

My brother, Scott, and Dad with their buck (1992)

PUT OTHERS FIRST

Philippians 2:3-4

"Do nothing out of selfish ambition or vain conceit, but in humility consider others better than yourselves. Each of you should look not only to your own interests, but also to the interests of others."

PUT OTHERS FIRST

I remember more fishing trips than all other childhood outings combined. Fishing was an inexpensive family activity that helped put food on the table. We had a white, aluminum boat powered by a small outboard motor. My father always sat in the last bench seat of the boat so that he could be in full control of the motor. My sister, Jill, was always stationed up front; her job was to look out ahead of the boat for hazardous rocks or stumps that might be jutting up and out of the water. I was always envious of her spot, as I sat in one of the two middle bench seats with my mother and brother, Scott. On several occasions our medium-sized dogs tagged along, which resulted in a very cramped middle section and even more chaos in the boat.

Regardless of my seat, I loved the glorious feeling of the wind rushing through my hair as we traveled by boat across lakes to spots that I was certain only my dad knew about. He would cut the motor and then row quite close to areas of clustered cattails and lily pads. Upon reaching our final destination, he would ask that the small white anchor be lowered. He then worked quickly to adjust all bobbers to the proper depth. My siblings and I all learned to bait hooks and cast at early ages. Once we knew our pole was good to go, each of us would anxiously attempt to grab our hook so we could wind an earthworm back and forth through the hook to keep it securely in place. While this happened, the boat was a mass of crossed poles. We were not supposed to stand in the boat, so my father usually tried to orchestrate the initial casts. If the fish were hitting, any semblance of order quickly turned to bedlam.

Sadly, my siblings and I did not master the art of removing our caught fish until much later in life. Quite often, three fish would be simultaneously dangling in front of my father's face. He hurriedly removed them and re-baited the hooks. He knew that if he did this, there was less chance of one of us snagging someone else's scalp or catching an eyeball. He tried to put the fish in our metal fish basket, but often he would just place them on the bottom of the boat where they would flip and flop, scaring the dogs, and often, us as well.

When not removing fish, my father was usually trying to release a snagged line. All too often, one of us would mistakenly catch a tree, something on shore, or the heaviest weeds in the lake.

With all of the activity and responsibility, my father rarely put his own pole in the water. Although he loved to fish, it was more important that his children have a good time.

Upon returning home after each fishing adventure, Jill, Scott, and I loved to proudly show off our fish before we ran off to play. Our father was then left to clean our catch.

Lesson Learned:

My father embodied selflessness throughout his life. In accordance with scripture, he served others and did not strive to be served. He was a role model who illustrated that one's own desires and needs often must come second to another's. It is only logical to believe that dramatically positive changes would take place in our society if more individuals put others' needs ahead of their own

USE GIFTS WISELY

1 Peter 4:10

"Each one should use whatever gift he has received to serve others, faithfully administering God's grace in its various forms."

USE GIFTS WISELY

My father was a jack-of-all-trades and master of most. Truly, it seemed there was nothing he hadn't done or couldn't do.

I can't remember when I first learned that he could knit. Likely, it was after I decided knitting was something I wanted to learn. Dad sat with me on the couch in our living room for many hours, needles in hand, trying to teach me the basics. Our problem was that he was left-handed and I was right-handed. I watched what he did and tried to do the same, only in the opposite direction. In the end, he learned how to knit right-handed so that I would finally catch on.

Eventually, I did learn how to knit in a straight line. With great delight, at the age of eight, I decided to make my father a scarf for Christmas. Each day, I would secretly work on the project using the sequence of knit two, pearl two. I was so proud to be using what I thought was a fancy pattern by incorporating the pearl stitches into the piece.

It was both a joy and relief to finally finish my masterpiece! With great anticipation on Christmas morning, I waited for him to open the big box that I had placed under the tree.

The look on Dad's face as he opened this present was unforgettable. Truthfully, he was shocked, but I thought he was surprised at my accomplishment.

Years later, with a set of "older eyes," I truly saw what my father did that morning many years earlier. The scarf was pale blue-green in color with fringe on the ends and measured at least six feet long.

But that Christmas morning he didn't say a word about the color, though I'm sure no man in his right mind, especially in 1966, would have been caught dead wearing pastel blue-green! The lovely fringed ends added to its decidedly feminine appearance, and with a long length, there was no discreet way to wear it under any outer garment. Still, in Dad's initial inspection of my stitches, he praised my work and graciously wound the scarf around his neck several times as we continued to open our presents.

That winter, I made sure that he left for work with his new scarf wrapped around his neck, though I'm sure it was lovingly placed on his car seat before he left the driveway.

Lesson Learned:

Although I did learn how to knit, my father taught me much more than a simple craft technique. It takes time and patience to be able to use our God-given talents and gifts to serve others. Praising another's work may be remembered for a lifetime, and receiving a present should always be done gracefully.

ADMIT YOUR MISTAKES

Colossians 3:13

"Bear with each other and forgive whatever grievances you may have against one another. Forgive as the Lord forgave you."

ADMIT YOUR MISTAKES

I always enjoyed recess. In third grade, every girl could be found playing hopscotch, jump rope, foursquare, or climbing on the monkey bars. I liked all four activities but was the least successful on the monkey bars. All I ever attempted was to cross bar by bar; skipping bars and swinging across was just not for me. It seemed, though, that all of my friends could skip bars with ease.

Well, one day I got the courage to swing, or quite possibly, I caved under peer pressure. All it took was skipping one bar. The next thing I remember is half sitting, half lying on the asphalt. My right wrist had taken the brunt of the fall. My being one of the larger girls in third grade didn't help the situation. My upper body strength was not what it needed to be to support my weight.

Upon entering the classroom, I approached Mrs. Loomis, bracing my wrist with my left hand. "I fell off the monkey bars and my wrist really hurts," I explained. "Can you move all of your fingers?" she asked. "I think so," I said as I attempted to move them while still bracing my wrist. "I'm sure it's not serious, but why don't you go and ask Mr. Bussle what he thinks." Mr. Bussle was the gym teacher for all grades. A classmate accompanied me as I walked to the gym. Mr. Bussle was standing near the gym entrance, so he had seen me coming. "Looks like you've got a sore hand," he remarked. "No, it's my wrist that hurts. I fell off the monkey bars and landed on it." He asked me not to brace the wrist as he examined it. "I don't see any swelling and it's not bruised. You sprained it."

I returned to class and wrote/scribbled with my left hand for the rest of the day and anxiously waited for the school day to end. When I got home, I was relieved, certain that my parents would make my wrist feel better.

My father listened as I described the fall and the degree of pain I was experiencing. He gently lifted my right wrist. "I don't see any signs of serious injury, Lori." "It really hurts, though," I reiterated. "Sprains can hurt pretty badly. It will get better," he stated. I walked away believing my wrist would most likely feel better by morning.

For the next two days, I wrote and ate with my left hand. Recess wasn't fun, since I now couldn't participate in any of the activities. I tried to support my right wrist as often as possible with my left hand and waited for the healing Dad had promised.

The third day after the fall, my father decided it was time for me to see a doctor. Before we left our house he said to my mother, "We'll settle this once and for all." I didn't understand what he was talking about, but I would soon enough.

As we entered the local Catholic hospital, an elderly nun asked what had happened to my wrist. I told her of my fall off the monkey bars and she immediately exclaimed, "Oh you must not be a very good monkey!" She laughed quite loudly as she shared the comment with surrounding strangers, oblivious to my utter embarrassment.

After the x-rays were taken, Dad and I waited in a small waiting room. A short time later, a doctor called out, "Mr. Campbell?" My dad rose to his feet, and I followed. "Mr. Campbell, your daughter has a broken bone in her wrist. We need to put on a short-arm cast." My father looked shocked, as his face turned beet red. "I'm sorry I didn't bring her in sooner; I thought it was just a sprain." Dad stood silently as the wet casting bandages were placed on my forearm.

I don't remember much about the ride home, but I do remember what happened when we entered our house. Jill thought my cast was cool and couldn't wait to sign it. Mom looked just as shocked as Dad had at the hospital. "Yup, Susie---it's broken," confessed my dad.

Dad looked straight at me. "Lori, I'm sorry for not taking you to the doctor sooner." Mom then spoke. "Mrs. Loomis called the day you fell and said you were probably exaggerating a bit since another student in the third grade has a cast, and everyone seems to want one. I told your dad about that phone call before he looked at your wrist that night." My dad shook his head and stated he would never let a teacher's beliefs cause him to doubt one of his children again.

As I entered the classroom the next day, Mrs. Loomis smiled as she looked my way. Instinctively, I raised my right hand, acknowledging her. When she noticed the "cast waving hello," her smile disappeared as her face suddenly matched her beautiful red sweater.

Lesson Learned:

As parents we're bound to make mistakes; we're not God. I was not a child who would complain of pain unless something really hurt. Although my father knew this, he didn't follow his instinct. He did, however, teach me the importance of recognizing a mistake and apologizing for it, even if it means apologizing to your child.

Dad never again doubted my siblings or me, and in fact, stood behind our word when others did not. Knowing that our father would and did stand behind us motivated us to be truthful so as to never lose his trust.

OBEY THE RULES

Hebrews 13:17

"Obey your leaders and submit to their authority. They keep watch over you as men who must give an account. Obey them so that their work will be a joy, not a burden, for that would be of no advantage to you."

OBEY THE RULES

One particular weekend day, my dad decided to go fishing on a lake several miles from our home. I don't remember how I ended up tagging along, but it was just the two of us who ventured out on that drizzly morning. I didn't mind that I had to wear my red oversized raincoat since I had been told that fish bite when it's raining.

Hours later, we didn't have one fish on our stringer. I'm not so sure we had even had one nibble, let alone a strike. My dad decided it was time to call it quits, and we motored for shore. He cut the motor quite a few yards from the landing and began to slowly row us in. I cast my little aqua Zebco, hoping for just one bite before we were off the water.

Suddenly, a third of my pole was bent down in the water. I couldn't lift it out. This was not how I wanted to end this fishing trip. "Dad, I think I've snagged my line," I sheepishly admitted.

No sooner had those words left my mouth, when my reel started to make whirring noises. My father immediately quit rowing, threw down the anchor, and informed me of what I now knew. I had a fish on this line and by the look of things, it was a big one.

"Here, Dad, take the pole," I pleaded as I motioned to give him the bent rod.

Smiling, he said, "No, Lori, you need to bring this one in on your own. This will be your fish story to tell. Just try to get your pole out of the water. You need to get the tip up!"

My arms ached as I braced the reel end of the pole against my abdomen and pulled with every fiber of strength I possessed. Reeling this fish in was next to impossible. I cranked the reel, at best, a quarter of a turn at a time. I was sweating and wished that I could remove my insulated raincoat, but that certainly was not going to happen.

"Keep cranking, Lor. Don't give up. Keep that line tight," he instructed.

My father and I became "the show" everyone wanted to watch. Fellow fishermen and individuals on shore were all watching as I desperately tried to hang on to this fish.

After what seemed like an eternity, I could see this fish fighting its way through the water as I inched it closer and closer to the boat. I was re-energized after catching sight of its size. I had never seen a fish this large except for the ones tacked up on the walls of my favorite restaurant in northern Wisconsin.

Sadly, we were a little unprepared for a fish of this size. We didn't have a net with us, so I knew that it was not going to be easy getting this one into the boat.

"Dad the line is so tight, I think it will snap if you try to grab it," I frantically declared.

Without answering me, my father quickly made a lunge for the line and grasped it. I always considered my father to be strong, but this would be a Superman kind of stunt. As Dad grasped the line, he immediately hoisted it upward and angled it toward the inside of the boat. I had been clutching the pole as tightly as I could. I couldn't bear to watch any longer. Suddenly, I felt droplets of water hit my face and the boat rock to one side. I opened my eyes. There were now three of us in the boat. My dad, me and a muskie! I was speechless as I stared at this giant. People on shore and in other boats were clapping and cheering. Wow---did I have a fish story to tell!

I could tell my father's excitement was subdued. "Dad, what's wrong?" I asked.

"I'm worried it might not be big enough."

"What?" How could this enormous fish be too small, I thought.

"The legal size for a muskie is 30 inches, Lori."

"Well, how many inches long is mine?"

"I don't have a ruler or tape measure, but I know that a one dollar bill is about six inches long." My dad then proceeded to open his wallet and remove a one dollar bill. Laying the bill on the fish, he determined my muskie to be almost five bill lengths long. "Lor, it's about two inches short."

"Oh, who cares, Dad? No one will ever know."

Dad then pointed to all of the people on shore and in the boats. "They'll know, Lori. We could be fined for keeping this fish."

"Oh please, Dad---I'll hide it in my raincoat. We have to show it to everybody at home." Tears started to stream down my face.

"Lori, the fish has to go back in the water. It's illegal for us to keep it." With that being said, Dad gently slid the giant back into the water. I couldn't bear to watch as my muskie swam away from our little boat.

Silently Dad rowed our boat to shore. When we landed, he explained to the onlookers that the muskie was just a little short. "Oh that's too bad," one said. "Tough break," voiced another. I didn't want anyone's sympathy. I just wanted to go home.

Dad decided to stop at his parents' home, which was located near the lake. My grandparents had fished the majority of their lives, so they would understand the heartache of releasing a catch such as this. I will never forget my grandmother trying to comfort me as I lay on her sofa. Wiping away my tears, she scolded my father for not trying to stretch the tail or lower jaw to add length. Sadly, her comments only made me feel worse, as my disappointment quickly turned to anger.

My father did not apologize for demanding that the fish be released. He maintained that it was the right thing to do. He couldn't convince me, but then again, I was only eight years old.

Lesson Learned:

Children's pleadings or tears can often influence a parent's decision. My father was not one to be swayed by either. By upholding his decisions, he taught me that doing the right thing is not always the easiest or most popular thing to do. I also learned that a one dollar bill is 6 inches long, which has come in handy on a couple of occasions.

I've never caught another muskie, but I feel so privileged to have caught one in my lifetime. I didn't return home with a fish, but as you can see, I did hang on to my "fish story."

MAKE IT RIGHT

Proverbs 16:11

"Honest scales and balances are from the Lord;
all the weights in the bag are of his making."

MAKE IT RIGHT

My father was always good with numbers and mathematical calculations. I stood in awe as he mentally calculated percentages regardless of the numbers involved.

Whether it was a grocery store, department store, or restaurant, my father knew our expenditures before the clerk or waitress could even reach a total. He caught numerous errors because of his knowledge of what the bill should be.

On countless occasions over the course of my life, I watched Dad graciously correct cashiers explaining an error had occurred, and he owed more than the amount he'd been billed. As a child, I could never figure out why Dad didn't just accept his good fortune and remain silent. As time passed, I noticed the gratitude and relief of the individuals after he corrected their mistakes. There were even times when Dad stepped in to help make change when cashiers became confused. He tried to teach them needed math concepts to perform this skill, as these were times before the fancy cash registers of today. He never said or did anything to embarrass anyone, he just tried to give "on-the-job training." Amazingly, Dad never lost his patience during these situations or complained about the length of time certain "errors" cost him. Most times as we left he would just say, out of earshot, "Poor kid."

In elementary school, I took great pride that Dad shared the same birth date of February 12 as Abraham Lincoln. Somehow, it seemed to make him important.

Years later, when I started to learn about "Honest Abe," I realized my father, whose nickname was Skip, shared more than just a birth date with Lincoln. Abraham Lincoln was seen as personifying honesty and integrity; the same held true for Dad.

Although he had very few mementos from his childhood or teen years, Dad did have one in his possession that impressed me, even as a small child. Though it hangs in my home today, it hung on a support beam in our unfinished basement, when I was a child. It is a large plaque with a detailed head and face on it; Dad made it when he was in high school. Perhaps the subject of the artwork was chosen because of his fame, his character, or that his birth date was shared with the artist. Whatever the reason, this piece of art is a true likeness of none other than Abraham Lincoln.

Dad's high school art piece

Lesson Learned:

One can speak of virtues but children learn best by witnessing virtuous behavior. I was taught that honesty is the best policy. More importantly, I was shown that honesty should be evident in every area of our lives.

Honest Abe helped shape this country because of the strength of his character. How fortunate for me that I was shaped by not only the words, but actions of "Honest Skip."

LOOK FOR THE LOST

Luke 15:4

"Suppose one of you has 100 sheep and loses one of them. Does he not leave the 99 in the open country and go after the lost sheep until he finds it?"

LOOK FOR THE LOST

My family was not musically inclined, though my father did have a "built-in banjo." He could make sounds with his mouth identical to that of a banjo being strummed. As children, we often begged him to "play his banjo," which almost always occurred when we were traveling in the car. Car rides also prompted the family to sing, especially our all-time favorite, "You Are My Sunshine."

That was the extent of our repertoire, so it probably surprised my parents when I came home from fifth grade pleading to take violin lessons at school. Since the lessons were free and I could borrow a violin, there was no reason not to try my hand at this stringed instrument.

Weeks into lessons, a Saturday practice was scheduled at the high school several miles from our house. Dad was unaware of my obligation as he ventured out early that morning to run errands. As practice time approached, my only option was to walk to the school, which required crossing a four-lane divided highway and finding a "shortcut" path that I had never taken.

Nervously, with my little black violin case in hand, I attempted the journey. I was relieved when I crossed the highways successfully and found the avenue with which the shortcut path intersected. I walked on the graveled edge of the two-lane avenue, first north and then south, hoping to find the beginning of the path, but I couldn't. I tried over and over, but soon it grew late, and I knew I would not be on time for group practice. This was not my biggest fear, though. Cars slowed in both directions when they spotted me. I worried that one would stop and I would be abducted by a stranger.

As my fears heightened, I heard a car slow down on the gravel behind me. My heart raced and I started to walk faster. There were no houses in sight, and I panicked, not knowing where to go or how to get away.

I would have run, but suddenly I heard a familiar voice. I stopped and quickly turned around. My fears vanished as I saw my father's friendly face poking out of the car window.

I ran to the passenger side, not even noticing the weight of my violin case. The sweet words, "Hop in kid," greeted me as I opened the door of our old white Ford. He had returned home from his errands to discover I was walking alone to the high school. Fearing I might be lost, he came looking for me.

What joy I felt as I sat next to him in the car! I had been lost, and unlike during games of hide-and-seek, I was so very grateful to have been found. He knew the way, and I no longer needed a shortcut.

Lesson Learned:

One of the worst feelings is knowing or thinking you are lost, especially for children. My father truly was my earthly savior that day. He came to search for the one who was not in the flock. Dad not only rescued me in the physical sense, but on more than one occasion he redirected me, mentally or emotionally, when I wasn't able to find my way. As parents, we should always be aware of our children's whereabouts. As human beings we should care enough to be our brother's keeper.

SYMPATHIZE WITH OTHERS

John 11:33-35

"When Jesus saw her weeping, and the Jews who had come along with her also weeping, he was deeply moved in spirit and troubled. "Where have you laid him?" he asked. "Come and see, Lord," they replied. Jesus wept."

SYMPATHIZE WITH OTHERS

My mother loved fish, reptiles, and mammals. As a result, despite growing up in the city, my siblings and I had a variety of pets; some were unusual to say the least. Dad was not as infatuated with our menagerie as Mom and we kids, but he tolerated it, rarely voicing a complaint.

In my elementary school years, I learned the names of various tropical fish, with guppies and tetras often being the most common in our aquariums. Betas were favorites, often contained separately in a glass vase or jar. Mom even brought home two newts once. They brought excitement to the aquarium and even more excitement when they escaped and were found days later desiccated on the kitchen floor.

Various birds also took up residence in our house over the years. Canaries, parakeets, parrots, and believe it or not, blue jays were all part of our family at one time or another. Mom rescued three orphaned baby blue jays and fed them with eyedroppers, raising them to adult size. They flew freely in our living room and kitchen scaring off relatives and friends alike.

Although I have never liked reptiles, chameleons freely roamed my mother's plants and occasionally "surprised" us by showing up on our shoulder or sleeve. Visitors did not find this entertaining and often asked about the small lizards' location before choosing a spot to sit and converse. Eggs discovered in a sand embankment adjacent to our house were *of course* placed in a dirt-filled aquarium in our kitchen. To my mother's and sister's delight, snakes hatched from these eggs. As they found joy in allowing the small snakes to wind around their fingers, I realized that I had not inherited my mother's *"reptile-loving gene."*

A couple of cats graced our lives, and we were never without a dog or two, or three, or more. Two separate litters of puppies brought the total to 13 at one point. Having other families adopt the puppies was nerve-wracking for all of us, including my father; he

One litter of Campbell puppies

was the one left to console each child and my mom as each puppy found new owners.

But, by far the most unbelievable pet was our goat, Heather. Remember, we did not live on a farm. Heather lived in our kitchen when she was not outside. She was as trained as a dog would be. When she grew to a size that was not suitable for "house" life, my mother found a home for her on a farm.

Each pet brought joy to our lives. Many also brought great sadness. I will never forget seeing my father cry while burying one of our beloved Airedale dogs. Mom, Jill, Scott, and I were mourning inside as Dad dug the deep hole needed to accommodate a large dog, outside. I peered out of my bedroom window, which afforded me a view of the back woods where Dad was digging. After each shovelful of dirt was tossed, Dad would stop and wipe his eyes. It was the first time I had ever seen my father cry. He was hurting just as much as we were over this dog's death. He had been trying to comfort us as we grieved. When he shed his tears, it was outside in private, or so he thought.

Dad with one of our Airedales

Lesson Learned:

My father was a sensitive man. He realized the passion my mother had for animals and supported her regardless of what awaited him when he walked through the front door every evening. It is wonderful for children to witness one parent supporting the passions of the other.

Dad was the pillar of strength supporting each of us through every trial and tribulation, whether it involved a pet or not. He had forearms like Popeye, and his hugs comforted everyone he embraced. Fathers need to hug their children and give them a sense of security regardless of the situation. Fathers should also never be afraid to cry or mourn, as children need to learn that grown men have feelings too.

MIND YOUR MANNERS

Proverbs 22:6

"Train a child in the way he should go, and
when he is old he will not turn from it."

MIND YOUR MANNERS

In sixth grade, I was proud to be a safety patrol member. I thought it was "cool" to wear the badge and be in control of one of the long crosswalk poles. It was even cooler to get out of class a few minutes early to perform the duty of ushering students across the street safely.

Each year, one safety patrol representative was chosen from each elementary school in the spring to go on an all-expenses-paid, chaperoned trip to Washington, D.C. Each school decided on its own how this lucky student would be chosen. At my school, the winner was selected by popular vote among the sixth-grade students.

Chances of winning were slim, but I still held on to hope. One could compare this to purchasing a lottery ticket, knowing there's *always a chance* of winning.

When the day came for the winner to be announced, I felt as if I had a giant knot in my stomach. We all sat at our desks as the long-awaited announcement was made. I closed my eyes and prepared myself to be happy for whomever had been selected. I'll never forget how it felt hearing my name called. I was ecstatic and speechless. It was the only "Miss America moment" I have had in my life.

My parents were just as surprised and thrilled when I told them I was the representative for my school. From that moment until the time I stepped on the bus headed for Washington, I was coached on how to behave, speak, and act while not in their presence.

Oddly, Dad seemed to be most concerned about dinner-table etiquette. He reminded me to put my napkin in my lap, keep my elbows off the table, and never to talk with food in my mouth. None of these "ideas" were new to me, but they bore new meaning as Dad seemed to have his eyes exclusively on me at the dinner table.

Along with basic table manners, he was determined that I learn how to properly cut different kinds of meat. I was accustomed to picking up chicken with my fingers, but this was no longer okay.

Dad wanted me to cut chicken regardless of the piece taken. Cutting the meat off of a chicken leg seemed ridiculous to me. It seemed only natural to pick a drumstick up and eat it. The worst "meat moment" was when I tried to cut a piece of round steak with a knife and fork and had the steak fly across the table because I hadn't "grounded" it with my fork. Dad just shook his head in disbelief as Jill and Scott roared with laughter.

He also made certain that I had the necessities for the trip. He showed me how to use the family camera and, afterwards, handed me five precious rolls of film for my big adventure. This was really a special occasion since our family did not take many pictures, as developing film was so costly.

When I boarded the bus in late May with all of the other sixth-graders from the area, it felt like I was beginning a final exam. I was as prepared as I could be.

On the trip, I did remember to put my napkin in my lap, and I tried not to talk with food in my mouth. I didn't order any foods that needed to be cut, because I didn't want to risk having something fly across the table. Although I tried to do everything just as I'd been coached, I couldn't understand why some of the chaperones and the waitress chuckled when I ordered fried eggs one morning. When asked how I wanted them cooked, I hesitantly said, "rare." Was there more than one way to fry an egg? All I knew was that eggs could be boiled, fried, or scrambled. This truly was a different part of the country to me.

When I returned home, I felt I had at least passed "the test." Mom and Dad listened as I recounted all of the trip details and seemed quite surprised, to say the least, to find out that I had purchased five additional rolls of film. When I explained that there were so many interesting sites to photograph, they seemed to understand. After the films were developed and four entire rolls were lovely shots of caged animals, they had somewhat of a different opinion. Our first stop on the trip had been the Washington, D.C. Zoo. What was a girl armed with a camera for the first time to do? Obviously, my lesson in "picture selectivity" took place at a later date.

Caged monkey (Washington D.C. Zoo, 1970)

Elephant (Washington D.C. Zoo, 1970)

Lesson Learned:

Dad's careful preparation and education of me was not so much for me to be a good reflection of him and/or my mother, but rather to be the best person I could be, regardless of my age or situation. It should be our duty as parents to train our children in ways that will benefit them "at the time" or "for a time to come."

Skills taught to the young tend to remain with them as years pass. For example, if a child learns to say please and thank you, celebrate when another wins, cut meat and have it remain on the plate, and/or pray to a God who listens, he or she will, most likely, not deviate from these teachings as he or she ages. Thankfully, I didn't.

Ceremony at Tomb of the Unknown Soldier (1970)

TAKE A STAND

1 Corinthians 15:58

"Therefore, my dear brothers, stand firm. Let nothing move you."

TAKE A STAND

The word "scab" took on a whole new meaning when I was a child. Instead of being a crusted spot on a knee or elbow, it became the name given to someone who crossed a picket line.

While growing up, my father and other teachers at his place of employment went on strike twice. Although Dad did not discuss much about the dispute in front of us, I knew he stood firmly in his position. I never really knew the issues surrounding the strikes, but Dad believed in voicing his opinion with a picket sign in his hand.

Secretly, I worried during these times. I was afraid Dad would lose his job, and we wouldn't be able to pay our bills. As our protector, our provider, our rock, Dad never voiced concern openly. If he did fret, it was done privately or possibly in the presence of my mother. He had taught us the futility of worry by using several phrases repeatedly over the course of our lives. He reminded us that worrying about tomorrow was for naught, since none of us was guaranteed that time or even the next five minutes. Anxiety over the past was covered with "Don't cry over spilled milk." Concern regarding any disappointment was met with the reminder that we should look at "our glass being half-full instead of half-empty."

Dad's demeanor, even in uncertain times, helped ease my fears. He never gave me any reason not to trust him, and so, I did.

Sighs of relief came when the strikes ended, and our lives returned to normal. I wanted to believe that there would never be another picket line, but my father taught us to "never say never."

I remember thinking that the scabs had been the smart ones, having never jeopardized their job security. In later years, I came to respect my father's courage and commitment during the strikes, as I watched him take stands on other issues.

He was not someone to sit on the fence or cross over the line. Fearlessly, he always stood his ground.

Lesson Learned:

Watching my father's commitment and courage over the years enabled me to take a stand on numerous issues without wavering or worrying. He illustrated that standing up for your beliefs may not always be easy or accepted. If we don't have the courage to stand for our beliefs, then we sit and our voice is never heard.

STOCK YOUR TOOLBOX

Proverbs 18:15

"The heart of the discerning acquires knowledge; the ears of the wise seek it out."

STOCK YOUR TOOLBOX

Most young children think their father is brilliant. I was no exception. Dad could answer questions on just about any topic and seemed to know something about everything. He also knew facts and figures. Numbers had a way of sticking in Dad's head. When Dad first shared that there were 5,280 feet in one mile, I sat in awe. How could he know that?

Dad's knowledge base was the reason I strove to do well in school. I didn't want to get good grades to impress him or anyone else. Rather, I wanted to do well because I wanted to know the answers to questions I might be asked, I wanted to know the answers to questions I might not be asked, and I wanted to effortlessly blurt out facts and figures. I wanted to be like my father.

To Dad, learning something new was like adding to a toolbox. Every subject or skill mastered was a "tool" that could be placed in one's personal box. Dad was quick to note that tools, left unused, might get rusty over time, but they would never be lost. Once a tool was in the box, it was there to stay.

Often times when Jill, Scott, or I would moan about having to learn a certain math concept or a seemingly unimportant fact, Dad would remind us that we were putting tools in our boxes. "You never know when a tool might come in handy," he would say. "It might be years before you have to take it out and use it. You'll be happy you have it then," he assured us.

Knowing the toolbox analogy at a young age gave me the desire to have one of the heaviest toolboxes around. I never shied away from difficult courses or tasks, so I collected a wide assortment of tools over the years.

Today, many of my tools are quite rusty, but it's comforting to know they're still in my box. Some have been cleaned up a bit and put to use tutoring my daughters in certain math and science courses. Others may never be used.

As I age, I realize how much room is still in my toolbox. There are so many things I do not know and so many questions I cannot answer. Although I always wanted to emulate my father, I realize that I will never match his knowledge or wit.

I will, however, keep adding tools to my box, in hope that it may one day be similar to Dad's…too heavy to lift!

Lesson Learned:

Knowledge is understanding gained through experience or study, which is reflected by the number of "tools" in one's box. Discerning individuals realize that with more tools, a greater number of projects can be attempted. Education in all forms, at any age, is beneficial. Subjects or concepts, seemingly irrelevant or unimportant, may prove quite significant at a later time. It is only by learning that we are able to teach. It is only by teaching that others can learn.

TREAT OTHERS KINDLY

Galatians 5:14

"Love your neighbor as yourself."

TREAT OTHERS KINDLY

My father had the dreaded task of teaching me how to drive a car. Although, I had the "paper" training and a few behind-the-wheel sessions at school, Dad taught the actual on-the-road lessons.

Somewhat "mechanically challenged," my attempts at mastering control of even a snowmobile left me less than confident; I managed to collide with small trees, shrubs, and even our house. I was content with passenger status when it came to enjoying our winter wonderland.

Driving an automobile was a different story; it was a necessity and a true rite of passage. I was determined to succeed.

Dad knew the best place for me to begin behind-the-wheel training was on country roads near our home. I'm sure he thought otherwise when I rounded a sharp curve and almost took three mailboxes home with us. With eyes as big as half dollars, he looked at me and quite calmly said, "That was a little close, Lor."

When we practiced driving in reverse, he said to crank the steering wheel in the direction the rear-end of the car was to go. Y-turns were easily learned, and coming to a complete stop at stop signs was a must, since Dad was not one to tolerate a "rolling stop." Parallel parking was my nemesis and an ordeal for my dad as well. He held his breath during these attempts, and since he didn't speak at these times, I always thought he was praying. In truth, I never actually practiced pulling in between two parked cars, as that probably would have warranted my father jumping out and directing me with arm motions or flares. But, I did pull up parallel to a parked car and maneuver in behind it. There was never another vehicle behind ours.

By far the most important driving skill Dad taught me was one he modeled every time he was behind the steering wheel. My father was the kindest, most patient driver I have ever known. He was one who always put pedestrians first, waited his turn, allowed other cars to enter his lane whenever the need arose, and excused other drivers' lack of skill or tact. I never once heard him raise his voice or curse at another driver or vehicle. His patience and kindness extended to me during the months he was my passenger, while I drove routes that became all too familiar to both of us.

In the end, tutorials enabled me to pass my licensing exam on a very snowy day. The thought of being tested when conditions were quite slippery was daunting. Ironically, when it came time for me to parallel park, the snow had gotten so deep that the licensor told me to forget it. What seemed like an environmental enemy had turned out to be my friend.

Lesson Learned:

I wish I could say that I am as kind and patient of a driver as my father, but truth be known, I am not. I do watch for pedestrians and allow other drivers to enter a lane when needed; however, I've been known to whip my right thumb in the air and shout, "Good one," when frustrated with other drivers' skills and or tact.

Still, when I "act out" in my car, I always think of Dad's calm and cool demeanor. He extended grace countless times without ever raising a finger---or a thumb.

BE MERCIFUL

Matthew 5:7

"Blessed are the merciful, for they will be shown mercy."

BE MERCIFUL

As many teen girls do, I went through a phase during high school of eating only what I perceived as healthy foods. I vividly recall eating cooked butternut squash on a school bus as the cheerleading squad was headed to an away game. Fruits and vegetables replaced typical teenage munchies.

One summer day after my junior year, my parents and I decided to enjoy a day of fishing on a lake only an hour from our home. As usual, it was Dad who gathered all of the fishing gear and poles, hooked the boat trailer onto the car, and tested the rear lights before we left.

It was a beautiful sunny day, and we were looking forward to this opportunity to be on the water. The radio was playing, and I was singing along as we headed north. It felt good to be out with just Mom and Dad. Dad stopped in an adjacent town to buy worms and get treats for us to snack on as we traveled. I was thrilled that he had specifically thought of me by buying several pounds of grapes in addition to chips and soda.

As we talked and laughed, I popped grape after grape into my mouth, until I suddenly realized there were but a few left in the bag. When we reached the boat landing, I knew I had a problem

Silently I stood by, watching as Dad followed the routine of getting our white aluminum boat into the water. After parking the car, he looked at me and noticed something was wrong. "Are you okay, Lor?" he asked. "No," was all I could say as I clutched my lower abdomen. "How bad is it," he empathetically inquired. With tears now forming in my eyes, I simply replied, "Bad."

Never in my life had I experienced such painful abdominal cramping. To make matters worse, there were no restrooms around. I felt as though I would soon explode.

Dad told Mom to jump in the boat as he helped me onto my seat. He then made a bee-line for the motor. Not one word was spoken as we sped across the lake full throttle. I pinched my thighs and bit the inside of my cheeks, not knowing if this mad dash would ultimately be in vain.

In record time, we reached a lakeshore bar and grill. Almost unable to walk, I made my way inside and headed for their restroom. After what seemed like an hour, I joined my parents, who were sipping soft drinks in the dining area. In just a few minutes Mother Nature called again. You might say she screamed. This went on all afternoon.

Our day ended many hours later with us crossing the lake, as Dad reversed each step he'd executed earlier in the day. He never once complained about the amount of time and effort involved in this escapade, or the fact that his line never even hit the water.

When we arrived home, he looked my way and asked, "How are you feeling now, kid?" Physically, I was greatly improved, but the guilt of ruining our day was overwhelming.

Hours later, the entire family laughed, recalling the day's events. I'd learned a valuable lesson: too much of even a "good" thing can be bad for you. Trust me!

Lesson Learned:

I did learn that overeating can actually lead to weight loss. But, more importantly, I experienced mercy at its best. Following my father's example, I have always felt compassion for those who are suffering.

My father never became flustered when plans went awry. He simply did what needed to be done, without complaining. When I was young, I naively thought this was "normal" behavior. Families would greatly benefit if more parents acted "abnormally," like Dad.

KNOW WHEN TO WALK AWAY

Proverbs 11:12

"A man who lacks judgment derides his neighbor, but a man of understanding holds his tongue."

KNOW WHEN TO WALK AWAY

I was not a rebellious teen, perhaps because I was more of a rebel in my younger years. Nonetheless, the teen years are never easy.

Although a cheerleader throughout junior and senior high, I was never part of the "popular" crowd. This was partly by choice, because I marched to my own drumbeat. Academics were important to me, and the party scene was not.

Cheerleading was an extracurricular activity I enjoyed that demanded hours of practice and performance. As a senior, I'd been chosen by the squad to be the captain. This was my second year as a varsity cheerleader, and I took this leadership position rather seriously; consequently, I didn't see eye-to-eye with my fellow squad members on many issues.

At the end of one late afternoon practice, two cheerleaders publicly criticized my personality and ability. Comments about my lack of enthusiasm and emotionless "performance face" were made. Even though I wasn't one to care what others thought of me, the attack still hit a raw nerve. As I was a returning varsity cheerleader, their comments were truly unwarranted and spiteful. I felt embarrassed, hurt, and angry. I sat silently, not able to utter a word. It was not that I couldn't have lashed back, but the lump in my throat prevented me from doing so.

Thankfully, it was the end of practice, and I exited the school before the first tear rolled down my cheek. My father picked me up that day and as I opened the car door, I saw the concerned look on his face. He was not accustomed to seeing me this emotional; he wouldn't put the car in drive unless I told him why I was crying.

Reluctantly, I told him what had happened. I explained, it wasn't so much what had been said to me but rather my inability to respond that had hurt so much. I sobbed as I shared with him how I had just sat and not spoken a word in my defense.

"Lor," he said, looking me in the eyes. "Some of the greatest battles have been won by silence." He believed I'd done the right thing by not responding.

In a brief moment, my father had taken this awful situation and made me feel like the victor. Not another tear was shed.

A couple of months after this incident, I suffered a major muscle tear in my right leg, which ended my cheerleading days. Nonetheless, I continued to march to my own drumbeat, albeit with a limp.

Lesson Learned:

How valuable to recognize that provocation need not be, and in most cases should not be, validated. A lump in my throat had kept me from responding, but in years to come, it would be the memory of my father's words that would help keep my mouth closed.

SUPPORT ONE ANOTHER

Galatians 6:2

"Carry each other's burdens, and in this way
you will fulfill the law of Christ."

SUPPORT ONE ANOTHER

I was one of those teenagers who studied diligently. My grades reflected the long hours I put in and were enhanced by my father's physics tutorials.

In my late teens, I'd decided nursing would be my future profession. I had no experience with the field, but I knew it involved caring for sick people and thought that I would be good at it. I had shared this career goal with several teachers during my senior year, and they advised me to consider becoming a doctor instead. At 17, I was flattered that others thought me so capable. From jump-rope days, girls were supposed to *marry* a doctor, lawyer, or an Indian chief---not become one!

Riding high on others' encouragement, I announced at dinner one evening that I was considering going to medical school after college. My father almost choked---literally. He then chuckled. I felt somewhat foolish as I told the family how I'd been encouraged at school to "shoot for the stars." Dad's face grew serious, and he said, "You have no idea what you're talking about." I wasn't so sure I did either, so the discussion ended---well, I thought it had.

Several evenings later, Dad approached me and wanted to talk. "Lor, I've been talking to a few people I know, and the idea of you entering college as a pre-med student isn't so far-fetched. You have what it takes to succeed academically if this is something you really want to pursue. I don't know how you would finance medical school, but whatever your decision, I'll stand behind it and support you in any way I can."

Not 100 per cent sure of what I was committing to, I answered, "I'd at least like to try, Dad." So, with his support, I did.

Lesson Learned:

I appreciated a father who took time to investigate a statement or situation if he questioned it in any way. Dad never chuckled again when I mentioned other dreams and goals. He stood behind me and beside me as I ventured on to "catch a star." His emotional, academic, and financial support enabled me "to try." And in the end, that's what was most important.

Dad supported me in many ways

TEACH WITH PATIENCE

Proverbs 16:21

"The wise in heart are called discerning, and
pleasant words promote instruction."

TEACH WITH PATIENCE

Some individuals learn to teach, and others are blessed with the natural ability. Some can teach one subject, and others teach in multiple areas. My father was gifted. He could teach anyone something.

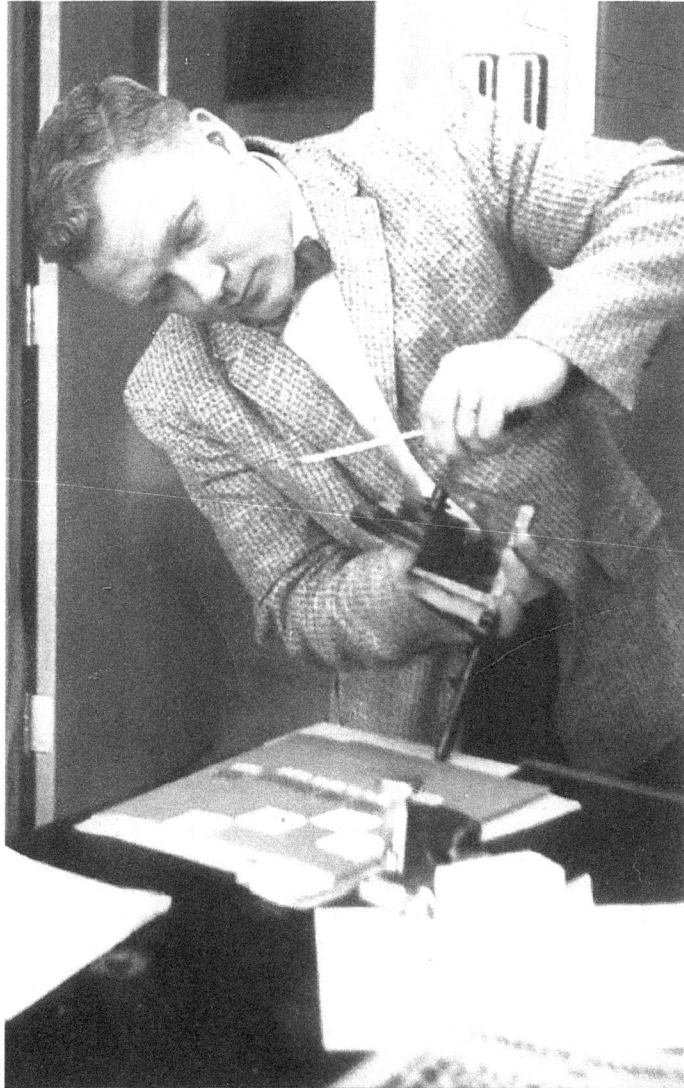

Dad giving a demonstration in one of the first classes he taught

All of those who teach should be blessed with a hefty dose of patience. Without patience, effective instruction is most certainly lost. Dad not only had patience, but possessed the ability to present subject matter in a variety of ways. He had a way of explaining complex issues in mathematics and physics, using simple terms and demonstrations.

I'll never forget struggling with rotational problems in calculus. I couldn't visualize in three-dimensional terms. My father tried multiple times to illustrate what was occurring with the different axes involved, but I couldn't get out of my two-dimensional box. Dad left my side only to reappear with a pencil and an orange. Tired and frustrated, I thought he'd lost it when he suddenly plunged the pencil into the orange. As he twirled the orange around the pencil, the door of my box finally opened. By observing that movement, I was able to apply it to the math problems that had perplexed me all evening.

Dad's skill at conveying basic physics was truly profound. Without his tutorials, I would never have passed my high school physics class. I tried to share what I knew with other students in my class, since it was apparent I had a "secret weapon" when test scores were revealed.

Amazingly, my father taught all day and yet truly never seemed to tire of teaching. He made time for his children if they needed help and always did so with patience, despite the late weekday hours when he was needed the most.

There came a point in time when my father could no longer help me out of my "boxes." Dad had given me roots in the fundamentals, which enabled me to develop wings to *eventually* fly out the door on my own.

I was blessed to have many great teachers over the course of my life, but none have compared to the one I consider the best---my father.

Lesson Learned:

Since my tutorial days, I've taught in a variety of settings and try to emulate my father's teaching style. I've tried to pass on fundamentals, which truly are overlooked in an age of calculators and computers. My daughters know that when it comes to math they had better never use a pen to do their work, and that it is vital to show all of the steps for a given problem whether one wants to or not. Regardless of the subject, I can still hear my father asking, "Did you read the book?" That question still echoes in the ears of my own children, too. Dad believed no question was too stupid to ask. More importantly, he never made the one asking the question *feel* stupid. Hopefully, my father's patience and teaching style will be passed down through the generations.

FINISH THE RACE

2 Timothy 4:7

"I have fought the good fight, I have finished the race, I have kept the faith."

FINISH THE RACE

My college life began at a large university two hours from home. The day I arrived, I carried a huge, hard-sided orange suitcase with all of my belongings--- everything but my lime-green bedspread. My roommate, a nice girl from a wealthy suburb, was not fond of my bedcover and desperately wanted me to use the extra frilly cover she brought from home, which matched hers. I think she wanted the room to look "coordinated." I graciously refused. This was not how I envisioned dorm life.

Classes were also not what I'd expected. Class size was large, and the atmosphere very impersonal. Worst of all, the lecturer of my favorite subject, chemistry, had such a thick German accent that I felt hearing impaired.

After two weeks, I decided this was not the environment for me. I wanted to study in a room by myself and feel as if my belongings actually "belonged." I wanted to go to a school where I could personally get to know my professors and not be known as "a number." I really just wanted to go home.

There was a pay phone in the hall of my dorm. It was my only hope of contact with the outside world. I reversed the charges and called home. After talking to Dad about my desires, he encouraged me to stay just a couple of more days. Two days later, I called again and repeated my wishes. Two days after that phone call, reversing the charges again, I told him that if he didn't let me come home I was leaving campus anyway.

At that point, Dad calmly said, "Come home." Looking back, he probably felt he had no choice. Perhaps, he knew he'd go broke paying the phone bill if I stayed. Whatever the reason, I felt okay knowing that Dad had given me permission to leave.

I got a job and worked that first semester while living at home. It wasn't easy. Relatives, peers, and friends found it ironic and rather amusing that the straight-A student couldn't hack college life. Although I never doubted my decision to leave, I doubted if I would ever be able to succeed in college again.

I don't know what I would have done without my father during that time. I know he'd been surprised when I decided to return home, but he never voiced disappointment in my decision or me. Dad encouraged me to look ahead and focus on starting my second semester at the local university. He reminded me that it did no good to look backwards.

That winter I started at the local college as planned, feeling as though I was now entering a race, laps behind the other runners. I was so afraid that I wouldn't be able to cope and would want to leave. I had no confidence in my abilities or myself. Each morning, my father would give me a pep talk and advise me to focus on just that one day---not the next or the next. He taught me the meaning of truly living in the present and not worrying about the future. He always said, "Just do the best you can, Lor."

After completion of the first set of exams, I grew more confident. It probably took at least two months for me to stop wondering whether I'd quit again. At the end of that semester, I knew I was capable of running "the race." Others were ahead of me, but my father made me realize that true success was not about how I would place but rather my ability to continue until I crossed the finish line.

Three years after that semester, I graduated summa cum laude with a degree in chemistry from our local university. I completed the race, came in first, and heartily embraced my favorite cheerleader at the finish line.

Lesson Learned:

Our children may make decisions that disappoint us, but it is important not to be disappointed in them as individuals. Hope is achieved by not allowing past failures to affect future achievement. The only way to finish a race is to have the courage to enter and to keep going---no matter what.

College graduation (Spring 1980)

EXTEND HOPE

Romans 15:1-2

"We who are strong ought to bear with the failings of the weak and not to please ourselves. Each of us should please his neighbor for his good, to build him up."

EXTEND HOPE

There were several semesters in college when I took heavy credit loads with an emphasis in chemistry and math. Many of the courses required a lab as well, so it seemed I was always busy. Although I tried to keep up in all of my classes there were times I had to "rob Peter to pay Paul." But, the worst heist of my life occurred when I "stole" from a mathematics course entitled, Differential Equations, to "pay" for University Physics and Biochemistry.

I found myself facing an examination in Differential Equations, having not kept up with assignments for weeks. My professor knew I was quite behind, as earlier in the week, I'd elected to "throw out" a quiz he'd given. At the beginning of the semester, this professor stated that each student would be allowed to discount one quiz. Well, without even attempting to take the quiz, I turned it in blank and told him this would be the quiz I would omit from my record. "If you can't do the problems on the quiz, you have no hope of passing the exam," he said. Though these words frightened me, I vowed to prove him wrong.

The evening before the exam, I told Dad my plight. He looked a little surprised and asked if I thought it possible to prepare in time. "Honestly, Dad, I don't know, but I've got all night to try," I replied.

To prepare for the test, I decided to do every assignment I'd not done over the previous weeks. Page by page, problem by problem, I read and solved. Although I worked as quickly as possible, this was not simple math. At one o'clock in the morning, I had a twinge of panic. I was tired and began to doubt my ability to complete all of the work and know the material before class time later that morning.

Around this time, Dad opened my bedroom door and put a big bowl of peanuts on my desk. "Brain food," he explained, then asked "How is it going?" I could tell by the look on his face he thought I'd committed "grand larceny." He typically didn't stay up this late, so I knew that he was trying to support me by staying awake, albeit in another area of the house. Although it would be a sleepless night for me, I encouraged him to go to bed.

As he closed my door, I wanted nothing more than to break down in tears. I probably would have if I could have spared the time, but I couldn't, and my eyes were tired enough already.

As young children, my father had taught us that one couldn't be afraid and eat at the same time. He would give us graham crackers during thunderstorms and his trick always worked. Well, I can tell you that the bowl of peanuts came at just the right time. I took a deep breath and popped a few peanuts in my mouth as I proceeded to do the next assignment.

It's a good thing Dad brought in a large bowl that night. I finished the last problem at approximately seven in the morning, just when I finished the last peanut.

My professor checked my exam before I left the classroom that day. I wasn't nervous because I knew I'd not just passed the test but had aced it. He looked at me, shook his head in disbelief, and asked what my secret was. I remember smiling as I passed him. "Peanuts," I said, under my breath, as I walked out the door.

Lesson Learned:

My father seemed to know what to do at just the right time. His "brain food" sustained me in more than one way that night. He had an ability to extend hope by simple acts. His sensitivity toward others always moved him to do what he could to improve any situation. Extending hope, in any way, prevents hopelessness and enables one to go on, regardless of the situation.

PREPARE FOR THE UNEXPECTED

Proverbs 15:22

"Plans fail for lack of counsel, but with many advisers they succeed."

PREPARE FOR THE UNEXPECTED

During my second year of college, I decided I would pursue my goal of becoming a doctor. When it came time, I applied to two medical schools and was granted interviews at both. Dad was kind enough to drive me to each. Both were hours away from my hometown.

Professors at college had given advice on what I should and shouldn't do and say. I purchased an inexpensive suit that I hoped conveyed an air of maturity and confidence, though I felt neither.

The day before my first interview, I packed a small suitcase with my essentials. I carefully hung my suit, covered with a long plastic bag, in the back of our family car. With everything loaded, Dad and I left right on schedule.

We stayed at a hotel that night, and I'm not sure I slept more than an hour. I kept thinking about potential questions I might be asked and was afraid I wouldn't know the answers. Quite frankly, I'm not sure Dad slept either, as this experience was uncharted territory for both of us.

When the alarm went off, I was already awake. I was nervous, but Dad's calm demeanor kept me grounded. I took several deep breaths as I started to get ready.

Everything went smoothly until I put on my nylons. My thighs had never been small and putting pantyhose on was a workout. I slowly inched them up with major struggles occurring above my knees. As usual, it felt like I was trying to stuff too much sausage into a casing even though I had bought a pair in which my height and weight fell well within the shaded sizing diagram on the back of the package. I wondered how women who bought this size, but were on the "outer edges" of the shaded area, ever managed to get them on. Finally, I succeeded in pulling them into place. My sense of relief was short-lived. As I looked in the mirror, I noticed a run in one leg that extended from the mid-calf up.

Panicked, I called for Dad, who was in the bedroom. When he heard of my dilemma, he merely said, "Don't worry. There's plenty of time. Just put on another pair."

"Who packs two pairs of pantyhose?" I asked myself. Since this was the first time I'd ever even packed one pair, I didn't know the answer to that question.

When Dad realized I hadn't prepared for a "mishap," his calm demeanor turned into a fright and flight response. He grabbed the car keys, pantyhose wrapper, and his wallet and quickly left the room.

I was a wreck. Dad, to my knowledge, had never bought nylons before, and where was he going to find a pair at 7 A.M.? If this incident was an omen, the outlook was bleak.

Dad returned, sweat on his brow, with two packages of pantyhose in hand. He was not about to take chances. I didn't think to ask where he'd found them. I just grabbed a package, ran back to the bathroom, and gingerly "yanked" them into place.

We left the hotel with only minutes to spare. Surprisingly, my anxiety level had decreased. I was relieved to be fully dressed and couldn't imagine what could happen that would be worse than putting on two pairs of pantyhose in one morning.

I arrived for the interviews on time and met with two male physicians who asked me a variety of questions. Upon leaving the medical complex hours later, I knew that whatever their decision, I had answered their questions truthfully and candidly.

I couldn't wait to jump back in our car. I was anxious to tell Dad my answers to their questions and even more anxious to remove my pantyhose and relax for the first time that day.

Lesson Learned:

Though my professors had advised me well, it was my father who made me realize that being prepared often means planning for mishaps to occur and not waiting until they do. Over the years, I've attended many professional meetings and events, and one thing is for certain-- you'll always find at least two pairs of pantyhose in my suitcase at all times.

DON'T BELITTLE DANGER

Proverbs 27:12

"The prudent see danger and take refuge, but the simple keep going and suffer for it."

DON'T BELITTLE DANGER

During spring and summer in Wisconsin, weather is variable; thunderstorms and tornado watches are common.

We lived in a split-level house on a hill. If the weather looked precarious, my father told us to head downstairs, as he monitored the weather from "his post." He sat on the steps leading to the main floor and watched the sky through two side-panel windows adjacent to the front door. As a family, we took tornado warnings seriously and followed the recommended guidelines. If the siren sounded, we would gather our pets, shoes, and the radio before heading to the basement… all of us except Dad.

July 15, 1980 was a particularly hot day. I remember it well, since it was my 22nd birthday. The temperature in the afternoon had been in the mid-nineties. Because of the heat, none of us felt like eating dinner. I only had an appetite for watermelon, so Dad went to the grocery store and bought the largest one he could find. It started to rain as he arrived back home, and trying to hurry inside, he accidentally dropped the melon on the driveway and it split into several pieces. Dad seemed a bit flustered, as he entered carrying the dripping chunks. We each grabbed a spoon and appreciated eating something cold and juicy.

The rain and wind picked up as we ate. We could hear the rain pounding on the roof and see the nearby trees swaying due to the wind gusts. Suddenly, we noticed the sky turning black. Dad got up and looked out the main picture window. The local siren began to blare at the same time Dad shouted, "Get downstairs!" By the tone of his voice, we knew he thought we were in danger. We yelled for the dogs, and they scampered behind us down the stairs. It wasn't until I saw Dad scurry to the basement, that fear gripped me. My fear only heightened as he quickly overturned our old sofa to form a protective barrier over our heads.

The wind hissed and howled and the house creaked. The rain pelted the windows with such force that I wondered if they would shatter. I closed my eyes and silently prayed. I could hear objects hitting against the house and wondered if it could take such a beating.

We sat huddled underneath the old sofa for what seemed like hours. As the wind died down, Dad ventured out of the basement to take his post on the stairs. I trusted his sense and knowledge of the weather, so I took his departure as a positive sign. We could rest knowing our house was still intact.

Some time later, we were given the okay to return upstairs. We were without electricity, so Mom lit candles in the living room and kitchen. Relieved, we joked about me not having a typical birthday celebration with cake and ice cream. My birthday was celebrated eating a smashed watermelon, sitting underneath an old sofa, praying for my life and holding a candle I couldn't blow out.

Straight-line winds reaching in excess of 100 mph had caused extensive damage to our community. It is on record as one of the worst storms in our town's history. It is also the only time Dad accompanied anyone to the basement.

Lesson Learned:

Dad's internal radar and sense of danger always gave me a sense of security no matter where we were. I also taught my children to appreciate weather and its changes, but unlike my father, I didn't man a "watchtower" during severe storms. I took the easy way out and just headed for the basement.

HELP MEET NEEDS

Matthew 5:42

"Give to the one who asks you, and do not turn away from the one who wants to borrow from you."

HELP MEET NEEDS

To provide for our family, Dad taught school during the day and sold insurance when not in the classroom. There was never a huge surplus of money in our home, but our needs were always met and desires almost always satisfied.

At Christmas, Santa brought many of the things we wished for, though he seldom left anything for Mom or Dad. As a child, that didn't bother me. I believed only children's names were on Santa's list.

As teenagers, Jill and I each got $50 as our present from Mom and Dad. We saved it to spend at a JC Penney Outlet Store that was about two hours from home. This store had bargain prices, so it made the trip worthwhile. I'll never forget the year we went in the dead of winter with no working heater in our family car. I can't remember if we left in snowmobile suits or purchased them at the store, but I do recall passengers in other vehicles looking at us as if we were aliens, dressed as we were, with our windows icy and fogged. Our feet were so cold when we arrived, that I questioned whether stretching our dollars was worth losing a few toes to frostbite.

Those years of post-holiday shopping inspired me to truly try to make my money go as far as possible. Bargain prices aren't affordable however, when you find yourself having no money.

That was never more apparent than during my first year of medical school. Although accustomed to academic rigor, adjusting to a new city, an apartment, and various social relationships was at times, more than stressful. To make matters worse, I hadn't received many loans my first semester, so money was extremely tight. I remember debating whether or not I could afford a carton of milk in a machine on campus. I finally decided I couldn't. Ramen noodles and JELL-O were my routine entrée and dessert, as I tried to pinch pennies wherever possible.

All was status quo until the day I was literally pinching two quarters. Those two coins were all I had to live on for the next two weeks. Frustrated and anxious, I called home and told Dad. It was not an easy call to make because I knew he would sell his shoes, if needed, to help out.

"How much do you think you need, Lor," he asked.

"Any amount will help," I replied.

"I'll make sure you get some in the next couple of days," he said.

As I hung up the phone, I questioned whether this career path was worth the time, energy, and money involved.

Two days later, as promised, an envelope arrived. In it was $100. Tears welled up in my eyes as I looked at the five crisp $20 bills. I knew Mom and Dad did not have this kind of money to spare. I vowed I'd never ask my parents for financial assistance again, and I didn't. But that didn't stop Dad from slipping me a few dollars every time I came home.

Dad was one to help meet any need. He invested time, energy, and money in my education and me. It was only fitting that his surname, through me, have the initials M.D. behind it. So, when I did marry, keeping my maiden name was my *only* option.

Lesson Learned:

I could never repay all that my father has given me, and he wouldn't want me to. He would want me to help meet the needs of others whenever and wherever I can. Whether it be holding a door for someone or giving a needed monetary gift, he would expect that of me and my siblings. When it comes to helping others, he would want us to "act out." There should never be *random* acts of kindness---just acts.

Dad and me (Winter 1981)

ACCEPT WITHOUT JUDGMENT

Romans 15:7

"Accept one another, then, just as Christ accepted you, in order to bring praise to God."

The Campbell Sisters

The Campbell Sisters (ages 2 and 5)

ACCEPT WITHOUT JUDGMENT

My father always accepted me for who I was. That's not to say he always accepted my behavior, especially when I was a young child.

He also did not ever compare me to my older sister, Jill. He understood we were two very different girls. I think Dad was aware of the differences from the moment he had to try and soothe his colicky second daughter.

Jill was athletically inclined; I was not. She fearlessly dove from the high dive at age 8, while I was "fished" out of the water, unable to complete a full length of the pool when I was six. That experience traumatized me so much that I did not go near a pool until age 12 when swimming was mandatory in seventh grade gym class. Jill and I were each given a pair of wooden red skis one Christmas during our pre-teen years. She excitedly rushed out to try them on our back hill, whereas I preferred to admire mine indoors. Jill was not one to shy away from trying new things; I, on the other hand, did not want to make a fool of myself attempting activities I had already decided I could not do.

Jill was also a gifted actress. At a young age, she appeared in multiple theater productions at our local university. In sixth grade, she landed the role of Dorothy in *The Wizard of Oz*. Although I didn't audition, I was asked to assume the role of a munchkin, who would have no lines. I must admit that in third grade I looked like a munchkin, being somewhat chubby and round-faced. While I physically fit the part, I graciously declined the only theatrical role that would ever come my way.

Dad never pressured me or my siblings to study or get good grades, I just did. He accepted the fact that my academic record was important to me and helped me perform to the best of my ability. Though he encouraged all of his children to study, he never rewarded classroom achievements with anything more than the words, "Good job."

Academics became my life as I ventured through college and medical school. He accepted the path I chose, and accepted my siblings' individual choices as well.

When it came time to marry, Dad readily accepted my fiancé, though it must have been difficult. My future husband, Bill, had been married once before and was on a military scholarship while attending medical school. My father had served in the United States Air Force during the Korean War. He and my mother had lived away from their families while fulfilling tours in Kansas and California. I had rejected military scholarships for medical school, in part, due to discussions with Dad. He advised maintaining the freedom to choose the location where I would ultimately serve as a medical doctor. Ironically, here I was, three years later, committing myself to Bill, who was legally bound to go wherever he might be ordered to go. When those orders did arrive five years after we were married, it was my father who encouraged us throughout the transition to military life in Hawaii.

Dad was surprised when I chose the field of dermatology for my specialty. I truly believe he felt that dermatologists were nothing more than "pimple pickers." I did, however, enjoy this particular area of medicine and the patients I was able to help. Still, I always felt torn between my home life and my professional life. Although I had studied long and hard for this role, I realized after a short time of practice that I was not suited to play it. Eventually I made the difficult decision to quit. When I walked off the set of *Dr. Campbell, Medicine Woman,* I'm not sure my father fully understood, but he accepted my resignation and remained a loyal fan, despite the "show's cancellation."

My father has been a constant source of encouragement and motivation during my journey on the yellow brick road of life. He has treated "the munchkin" just like "Dorothy," despite our differences. He understands that many roads lead to Oz. It is good that I don't need a pair of ruby red slippers to return home---my place of acceptance and grace.

Lesson Learned:

My father did not compare one child to another. He recognized and accepted differences in each of us. We flourished because we were treated as individuals. His acceptance of our decisions illustrated his trust in us. By him trusting us, we learned to trust ourselves.

Jill and me on my 50th birthday

DON'T SWEAT THE SMALL STUFF

Matthew 6:27

"Who of you by worrying can add a single hour to his life?"

DON'T SWEAT THE SMALL STUFF

The January of my third year of medical school, I got engaged to my classmate, Bill. He appeared at my apartment with a small bouquet purchased from the hospital gift shop. I was thrilled to say, "Yes!"

We decided to marry that summer. Our break from school was not long, and two couples from our class had already chosen two of the three available weekends. Only the July 4th weekend was left. We opted to take it and started to make plans.

I was concerned about all of the details, but Dad kept reminding me that in the grand scope of things, the wedding was not a big deal. "What's important, is to know that you have found the one you want to commit your life to," he reminded me. "The flowers, cake, and dress are really just fluff," he said.

I tried to relax, but with my hectic schedule and living three hours from home, it was not easy. The weekend I was to go dress shopping, my mom was diagnosed with pneumonia, and my sister wasn't able to make it. Dad offered to go with me, but I decided to take Bill, as he knew the dress style I was looking for. The salesperson at the bridal shop could not believe that I brought my fiancé to look at dresses. She was even more baffled when Bill found a dress on the rack and said, "Lori, I think I found one you'll like." Minutes later, after trying it on, I purchased that dress. The poor saleswoman was speechless.

That same weekend we secured a reception site, ordered the flowers and cake, and hired a photographer. As we left to return to school, Dad said, "See, Lor, there was nothing to worry about."

I was so busy over the next five months that I truly spent little time thinking about the wedding. My only daydream was thinking about what it would be like walking down the aisle with Dad. I had always envisioned being on his arm and calmly talking and smiling as we neared the altar.

The day of the wedding was hot and humid; it was so hot that one of my distinct memories is watching the sweat droplets cascade down the minister's nose and fall onto his Bible. Since the church was without air-conditioning, it left much to be desired.

My two-year-old niece served as a tiny flower girl and had to be coaxed down the aisle. Jill, who served as my only attendant, followed her. Dad stood quite solemnly by my side as we awaited our grand entrance.

As my sister neared the halfway point of her walk, Dad suddenly left my side and exited the church. He mumbled a few words as he left, but having been so surprised by his movement, I couldn't understand what he'd said. There I stood, alone, not knowing what to do. A dear classmate, who was serving as an usher, asked if he should escort me. I quickly decided that when the designated song began, I'd walk alone.

As my sister reached her assigned position, I knew all eyes would soon be on me. Instead of panicking, I tried to focus on what was important---exchanging vows with the man I wanted to spend the rest of my life with.

Then, just as suddenly as he'd disappeared, Dad reappeared, quickly stuffing a handkerchief into his left pocket before wrapping his arm around mine. His eyes were red. It appeared the emotion of the day had overwhelmed him. Not wanting to add to those feelings, I walked briskly to the front of the church, never looking his way or speaking a word.

Bill stood perplexed; he knew something was amiss as he watched us somberly approach. I quickly took Bill's arm and proceeded to marry the only man I had ever considered as a lifelong mate.

We would later laugh about the events of the day. Dad said he was doing well until he saw his little granddaughter walk down the aisle. With emotions riding high, he knew he needed a breath of fresh air before escorting me. He apologized for leaving me high and dry at the back of the church.

There were other glitches on our big day that were also fondly recalled. Bill and I had concentrated so much on watching the sweat droplets "ski" down the minister's nose that we remembered little of

The infamous walk down the aisle

the ceremony. Our vocalists apologized for singing, "We should go out and *seed* the poor," instead of the intended words, "We should go out and feed the poor." Lastly, all of us roared at recollecting the last words of the service. Bill and I had been united in "holy wedknock."

The best planning would not have prevented the "errors" of the day. Dad had been right from the beginning. What was most important was the marriage---not the wedding.

Lesson Learned:

Dad had a way of putting things in perspective. He taught that worry never helps anyone or anything. He always put a positive spin on every situation.

Although my wedding was not what I thought it would be, it has brought countless laughs to many as I retell the day's events. For this reason, I couldn't have asked for a better day.

Smiles and laughter after the ceremony

LET GENTLENESS BE A STRENGTH

Philippians 4:5

"Let your gentleness be evident to all. The Lord is near."

LET GENTLENESS BE A STRENGTH

My father and mother held my first daughter, Claire, within hours of her birth. This was possible only because Dad was attending a meeting in a city one hour from where Bill and I were living on the day I delivered. We were in the third year of our residencies, and traveling four hours to Mom and Dad's house had been a rare occurrence in previous months. Seeing them walk through the door of my hospital room was a welcome surprise.

I remember lying in the hospital bed and watching Dad embrace the newest member of the family. I'd seen him hold other babies over the years, but now, I marveled at his natural ability to cradle an infant, my infant, in his muscular arms. Some men hold babies as if they're footballs, and others shy away or are awkward with the encounter. Only a select few are true gentle giants.

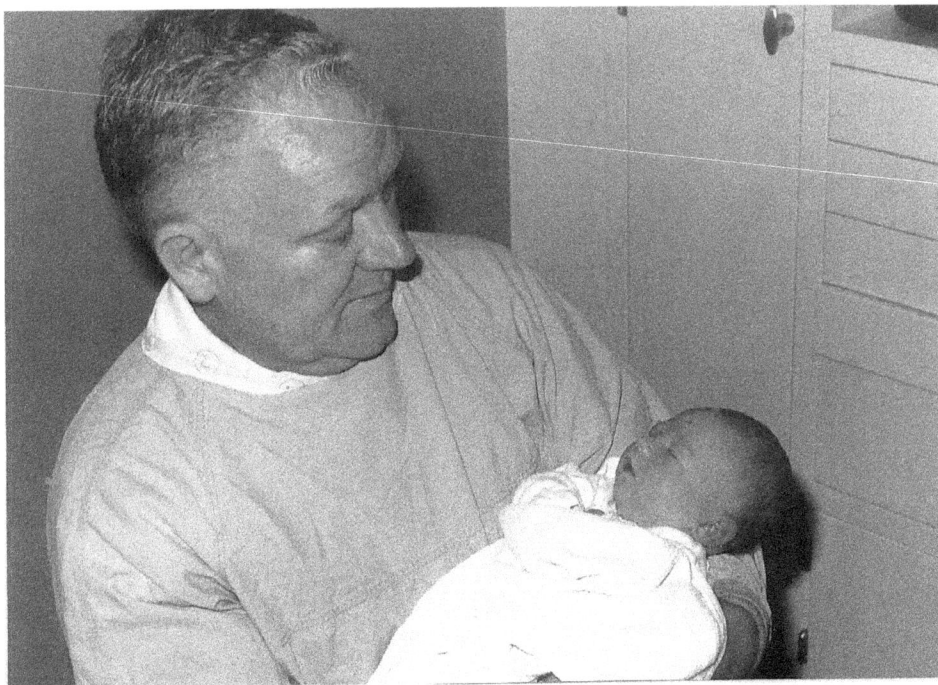

Dad and Claire on the day of her birth (10-11-86)

Dad was equally adept at picking up, setting down, and/or comforting infants. He was especially gifted at calming fussy or crying babies and toddlers. He would often walk endless miles around rooms with a small head on one of his shoulders while whispering sweet somethings into a tiny ear. Multiple snapshots in photo albums capture him carrying one of my daughters with her torso supported by one of his forearms as he rocked her, belly side down, with her tiny legs straddling his arm. It seems he'd mastered this technique when trying to soothe the most colicky baby of all 30 years earlier---me.

To this day, my girls are comforted by a song Dad often sang to them as he carried them into dreamland:

"Go to sleep, my little baby,

Go to sleep my little baby.

When you wake,

You patty patty cake

And ride a tiny little pony."

All it took was for Dad to start singing in his soothing low voice, and then their little bodies would relax and their eyes would begin to close. I believe Dad's gentle nature conveyed such love and security that each infant or child felt totally at peace.

That same love and security extended well beyond the infant/toddler years. Dad was always generous with hugs. Though there have been many times when I have wished Dad could pick me up and rock me in his arms, holding his hand or hugging him has always transferred his magical, gentle touch.

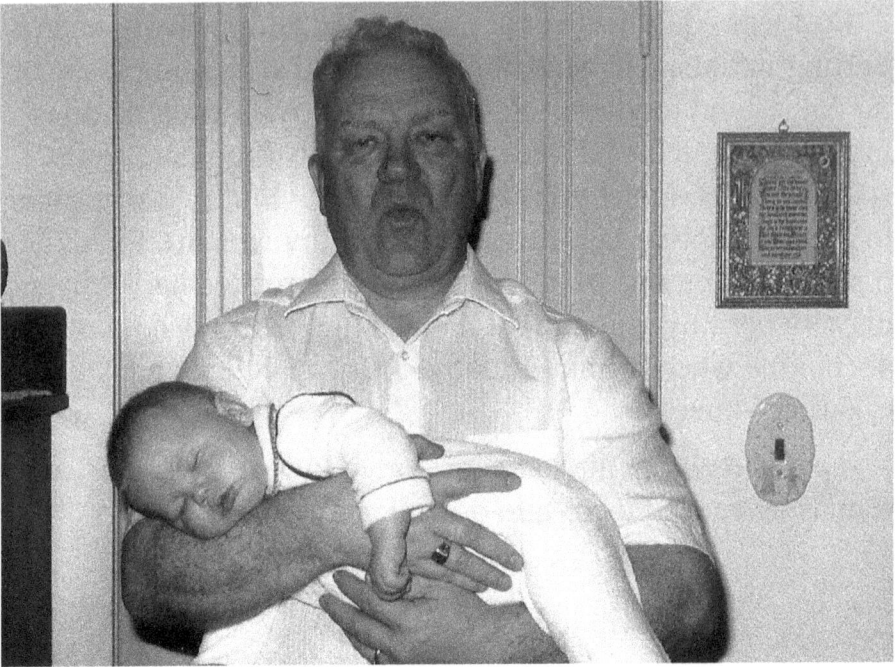

Dad and Claire

Dad and Maggie

Lesson Learned:

More often than not, society looks to females to be the tender souls in children's lives. While that's often true, I have come to believe that the true strength of a man lies in his gentleness.

One of Dad's generous hugs

SPREAD JOY

I Thessalonians 5:16
"Be joyful always."

SPREAD JOY

Dad seemed to put a smile on someone's face no matter where he went. His sharp wit caught many by surprise but always brought grins and or laughter. Dad's delight was in making someone's day just a little bit brighter. He held a firm belief that everyone needed to have "a little fun."

Fun was the last thing on my mind, when Claire and I moved in with my parents after the completion of my residency program. At that time, it was necessary for Bill to begin his military duties in Hawaii. I had elected to stay in Wisconsin, since I was scheduled to take my dermatology board examination, which was offered every fall in Chicago. That decision meant that Claire and I would live apart from Bill for five months in familiar, yet strange surroundings.

Our household goods had been either stored stateside or shipped across the Pacific, so Claire and I arrived for our stay with few clothes, toys, and books. Though Claire's welfare was my number one concern, I knew I needed time to review and study for my upcoming exam. I wasn't sure how to keep Claire entertained, but Dad had a few ideas.

Days after we arrived, Dad was beaming as he asked Claire to go outside with him. I peered out a back window and watched Claire excitedly jump up and down at the sight of Dad's acquisition---a previously-owned blue and white metal swing set. Dad was smiling as he hoisted his 20-month granddaughter onto the glider. That scene would repeat itself many times over the summer months.

A couple of weeks after the swing set purchase, it was my turn to follow Dad outside, upon his request. I was a bit perplexed to see his ice-fishing shanty set up adjacent to the set.

"What's going on, Dad?" I asked.

"Just follow me, Lor," he replied.

As dad opened the flap to the shanty, I stood in disbelief as I peeked inside. "Oh Dad, this is so cool! Leave it to you to think of something like this." Tears came to my eyes as I looked up into his radiant face.

Dad had turned the shanty into "Claire's Kitchen." Given the opportunity at a thrift sale to purchase used, child-size kitchen furniture, dad jumped at the chance. It was his creative genius to "install" it in a "private room" outside.

I will never forget Claire's joy at seeing her special space. Her squeals of delight made all of us laugh.

Claire enjoyed many hours outside that summer. If she wasn't playing on the swing set or in her kitchen, she was off feeding ducks at the local park with her grandpa.

As autumn and my exam date approached, my anxiety increased as the outside temperature decreased. Claire spent more time inside, which limited her activities and altered my study schedule.

Dad knew I was concerned about this final examination. It would be given over two days and covered years of published information and coursework as well as testing on multiple microscopic slides. A couple of weeks before the test date, Dad came up with an ingenious solution that allowed Claire to be outside more, thus giving me additional time to study.

Giggles and laughter led me to this final site of outdoor entertainment. Looking once again through a window, I saw Dad and Claire seated in our aluminum fishing boat securely attached to its trailer. Dad had obviously hauled the boat to the back yard with his truck and placed it within feet of the back door. He had decided to teach Claire how to cast using a small rod and reel. I stood for minutes watching the interaction between this familiar teacher and his 2-year- old student. It was surreal to watch my own little girl grasp the techniques I had learned so many years earlier from the same instructor.

Within a short time, Claire was successfully casting into a sea of fallen leaves and brown grass. Daily adventures in the stationary boat kept Claire occupied while I finished my review.

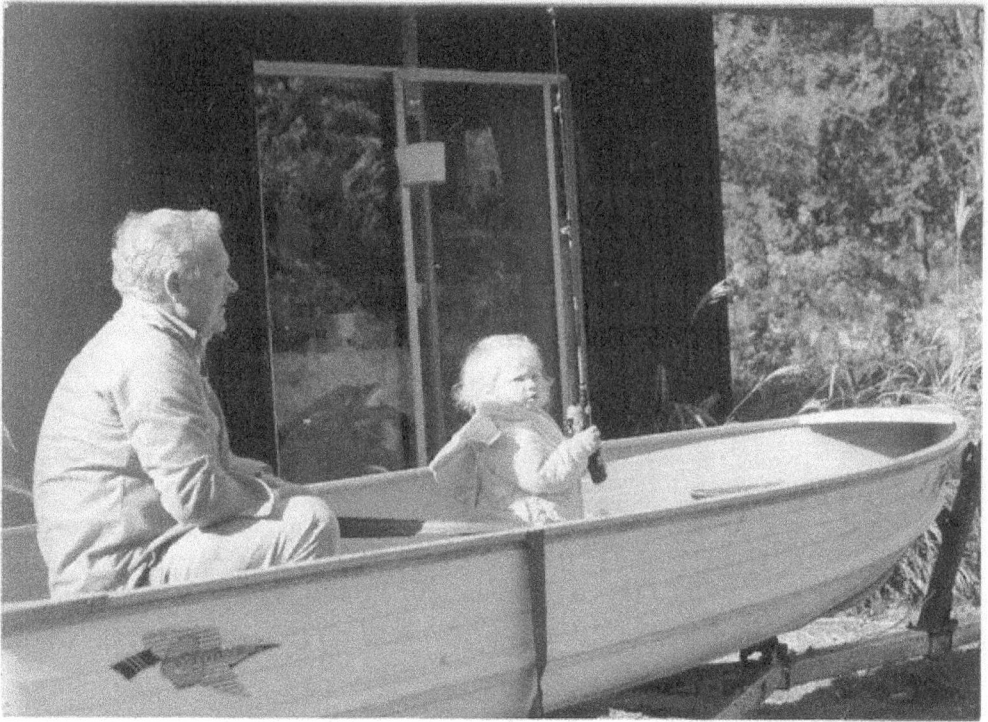

Dad teaching two-year-old Claire how to cast

The months of separation from Bill had been difficult, but Dad had managed to repeatedly generate smiles on my face and Claire's. I did pass my board examination that October and was so very grateful for all of the help I had received from my parents during our stay. Despite our situation, Claire and I had fun during our "displacement." We had been blessed with a heaping helping of joy that had been thickly spread over us by a man who wanted nothing more than a smile in return.

Claire (Summer 1988)

Lesson Learned:

We should strive to bring happiness to others. It doesn't take money or even a lot of time to put a smile on someone else's face. In delighting others, we will bring delight to our own souls. The more joy we give away, the more joy infuses into our own being until we exude it, as my father did.

Dad bringing another smile to Claire's face despite not actually knowing how to play an accordion

TAKE WHAT YOU GET

Philippians 4:12-13

"I know what it is to be in need, and I know what it is to have plenty. I have learned the secret of being content in any and every situation, whether well fed or hungry, whether living in plenty or in want. I can do everything through Him who gives me strength."

TAKE WHAT YOU GET

Two years after Claire was born, we moved to Oahu. Four months after we arrived there, I learned I was pregnant with our second child, and I was happy to be fulfilling my duties as a full-time M.D. (Mother Dear) for the first time.

Initially, it was difficult adjusting to living so far away from family and friends, but morning sickness quickly outweighed my homesickness. In addition to the nausea, I began to experience frequent episodes of erratic heart rates. I had experienced similar rapid heart rhythms during my first pregnancy, but Bill and I never worried since we had self-diagnosed my condition as nothing more than a nuisance. With the second pregnancy, the episodes were occurring daily and lasting 10 to 15 minutes in duration, which alarmed both Bill and me.

Medical maneuvers sometimes stopped episodes, but they weren't reliable. Submerging my face in ice water, one such trick, often brought my heart rate down. I jokingly warned acquaintances that they might find me at the commissary with my head in a frozen food compartment.

After discussing the problem with my obstetrician, I was referred to a cardiologist who ordered a battery of tests. Opinions and diagnoses were offered. Concern was raised about my health and the health of our unborn child.

With hormones and emotions at their height, I called home and spoke with Dad. "What is your greatest fear about the situation?" he asked. "Dad," I tearfully replied, "We don't know if my abnormal heart rhythms have hurt the baby, and we might not know until the delivery." Without hesitating, Dad responded in a way that made me realize this news didn't change the outcome of what would take place when our child was born. He said, "It's this simple, Lor--whatever comes out, you're going to take it home and love it." I sat silently, absorbing the words he had spoken. He was right. I couldn't change what had already occurred. We were medically managing the situation to the best of our abilities.

At the end of that very long distance call, I wiped away my tears. Dad had reminded me that pregnancy is one of those times when one must be prepared to accept and love regardless of the outcome. My fears dissipated knowing that I could accept and love whomever I would meet in early October.

And, when the time came, I gave birth at Tripler Army Hospital in Honolulu, to a 9-pound, 10 ½- ounce baby girl. She was by far the largest infant in the newborn nursery. She was perfect in every way except her right foot appeared mal-aligned and underdeveloped; however, this was the result of intra-uterine positioning, and it corrected itself by the age of four months. Today, this 5-foot, 9-inch daughter is a bright, beautiful young woman, named Maggie. Maggie inherited my father's cleft chin, a feature she was never happy to have "received." I, on the other hand, am happy that her genetic "stamp" reminds me of Dad, who emphasized, before her birth, the basic premise that acceptance and love begin at conception.

Dad meeting Maggie for the first time (May 1990)

Maggie, the hairstylist, and her "client"

Lesson Learned:

It is human nature to want everything to be perfect, but we will never find or achieve perfection on earth. If we take what we get and love it, make the most of it, and feel content, then we will have done all we can and should do.

Claire, Mom, Dad, and Maggie (Christmas 2007)

COUNT YOUR BLESSINGS

Colossians 3:15-16

"Let the peace of Christ rule in your hearts, since as members of one body you were called to peace. And be thankful. Let the word of Christ dwell in you richly as you teach and admonish one another with all wisdom, and as you sing psalms, hymns and spiritual songs with gratitude in your hearts to God."

COUNT YOUR BLESSINGS

Living on the island of Oahu had its advantages. It was wonderful to be surrounded by flowers and sunshine most days of the year, and going to the beach was a common occurrence since we lived so close to the ocean. Not having to dress the girls in snowsuits and boots was a blessing as they lived in shorts and flip-flops. Eating mangos, guavas, pineapples, and/or papayas was a daily treat.

On the other hand, island life had its disadvantages as well. Since I never cared for chameleons as a child, living with geckos was not something I enjoyed. Often one would leap from the kitchen cupboards, and I would scream in fright. Once, one leapt onto my lap as I sat in the passenger seat while Bill was driving. I immediately tried to open my door to escape, while the car was moving, which caused quite a scene. I was also warned that gecko droppings look like raisins and are often salmonella-laden treats for toddlers. I was always on the lookout for pseudo-dried fruits. Complicating my life, the Hawaiian language, though beautiful, is difficult to read since multiple vowels are often strung together to make various words. Many times, if given directions, I could not spell or read the names of the streets involved because of their odd spellings. It truly was a "foreign land." Worst of all, living on a speck of land in the middle of the Pacific Ocean kept me isolated from my extended family. I sent letters, pictures, and videotapes back home, trying to keep them updated on our lives, but that didn't help on our end. We were missing all of the family gatherings, and it was heartbreaking. Phone calls were my lifeline to Mom and Dad and to the mainland in general. Each call soothed my soul and put a smile on my face, except for the call that came at the beginning of our fourth year away.

"Lori," Mom said. "Mom?" I asked. An uncomfortable silence followed. I could tell she couldn't talk. I knew something was wrong with Dad. "Is he still alive?" I asked, trembling as I stood in my kitchen within earshot of dinner guests. "Yes," she replied. I listened as she told me he'd been taken by ambulance to an emergency room for evaluation of upper abdominal pain. Paramedics had assured Mom that Dad was not having a heart attack.

Within minutes of hanging up the phone, Bill was speaking with the attending physician on call in the emergency room, thousands of miles away in my hometown. Dad's preliminary diagnosis was peptic ulcer disease. The tentative plan was to discharge him and schedule a barium swallow on a future date. Knowing my dad's stoic nature, Bill recommended Dad not be discharged without a full cardiac work-up. Bill knew that Dad would never consider going to a hospital, much less by ambulance, unless the pain was severe. Since upper abdominal pain can also indicate heart trouble, Bill wanted to make sure Dad's heart was not the cause of the pain. Because of Bill's advice, a cardiac stress test was scheduled for the next day.

It was fortuitous that I'd booked a flight home after the initial phone call. After 17 hours of air travel with layovers, I arrived back in my home state to find out the stress test results were markedly abnormal.

It was both a blessing and a curse to be the only medical professional in my family. When the cardiac catheterization revealed life-threatening blockages, I excused myself and emotionally fell apart in an adjacent hallway. I knew if Mom, Jill, or Scott saw me break down they would view the prognosis as hopeless.

Dad was to have bypass surgery within approximately 12 hours. I prayed to and pleaded with God to restore my father so that Claire and Maggie would be given the chance to know this remarkable man. I couldn't fathom losing him at the age of 59. I called Bill and sobbed uncontrollably on the phone. I felt helpless. There was nothing I could do to help my father, except pray.

As Dad was wheeled to the operating room, I was given his watch and wedding ring, since Mom had elected to stay in a separate part of the hospital while Dad was in surgery. Trying not to cry, I kissed him on the forehead and told him everything would be all right.

Overflowing with anxiety, I felt as though I would vomit as I took a seat in the surgical waiting room. I put Dad's watch on my wrist and held his wedding ring tightly in my right hand. I squeezed it in my fist, as if that act could somehow transfer strength to Dad. I felt as though I was about to hyperventilate, when suddenly there was a voice, not audible to anyone but me that said, "If I raised my Son from the dead, don't you think I can give you back your father?" Then I felt a wave of peace like I've never known. Not once did I question what had just taken place. God had spoken, and I knew Dad would make it through the surgery. I calmly sat, envisioning Dad in the near future, walking on the beaches I'd come to know and love.

Eight months later, that vision became a reality. After Dad's quadruple bypass, it was revealed that he had what is known as the "widow maker." He had silent left main coronary artery disease, which was so severe that saline (salt water) could not pass through this vessel during the surgery. There was complete blockage. Dad's survival was a miracle.

During my parents' visit to Oahu, a picture was taken of Maggie riding atop Dad's shoulders. Seeing this picture reminds me to be grateful each and every day. Maggie and Claire were *given* the opportunity to know my father. Each day I am grateful for Bill who, because of his advice, changed the course of Dad's medical evaluation and undoubtedly saved his life. I am also thankful for the cardiovascular surgeon, Dr. John Overton Jr., who had the knowledge and talent to successfully operate on Dad. He also had a bedside manner that soothed not only Dad, but all family members present. Most importantly, I am eternally grateful for an all-knowing God who spoke to me, reassuring me of Jesus' resurrection and my father's restoration.

Maggie riding atop Dad's shoulders (Spring 1992)

Lesson Learned:

It is so easy to take everything and everyone for granted. Though we know that life can change in an instant, it often takes a crisis for us to see with "grateful eyes." May we take time every day to count our blessings and be thankful for each one.

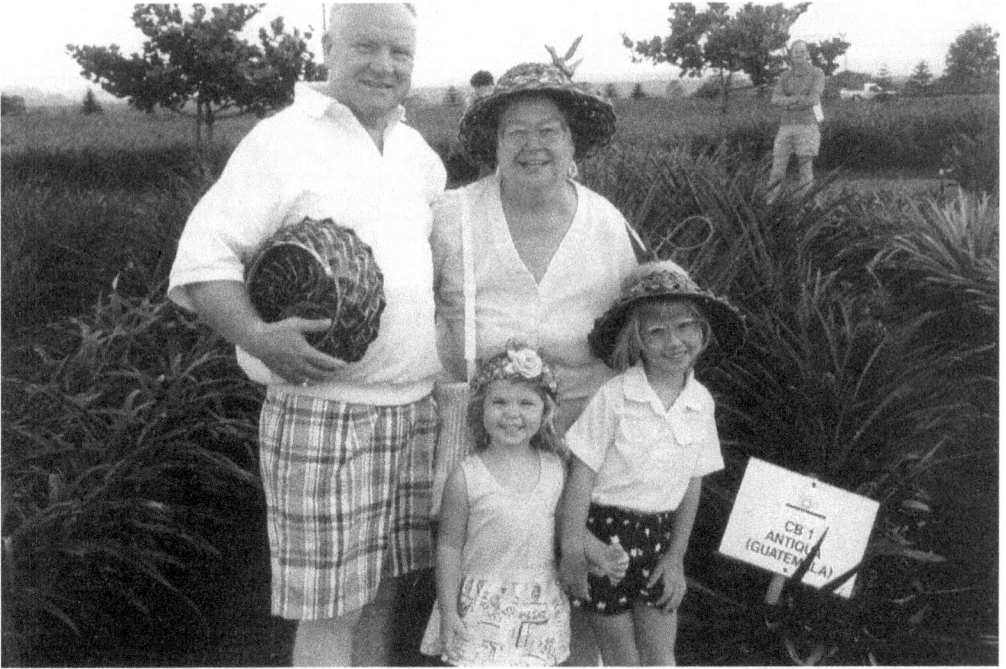

Dad, Mom, Maggie, and Claire at Dole Plantation (Spring 1992)

BELIEVE IN MIRACLES

Luke 7:12-15

"As he approached the town gate, a dead person was being carried out, the only son of his mother, and she was a widow. And a large crowd from the town was with her. When the Lord saw her, his heart went out to her and he said, 'Don't cry.' Then he went up and touched the coffin, and those carrying it stood still. He said, "Young man, I say to you get up!" The dead man sat up and began to talk, and Jesus gave him back to his mother."

BELIEVE IN MIRACLES

Months before Dad had quadruple bypass, I began questioning my spiritual beliefs. Brought up attending Sunday school, I'd been baptized as an infant, confirmed in the Lutheran faith, and raised Christian. I never doubted the existence of God. Studying medicine and the human body reaffirmed my belief that our "beings" were divinely created. My sudden struggle was with Jesus. Although I knew all about his life and death, I began to wonder, "How do I know that He was who He said He was?" The evening I shared this thought with Bill, he matter-of-factly said, "You know, Lori, you can believe in God, yet not be a Christian." I was livid. Was he implying I wasn't a Christian? After taking time to think it over, I realized he was right. By definition a Christian is a follower of Christ. Suddenly, I was frightened. Why was I questioning the divinity of Jesus Christ?

I needed answers, so I began to search. My minister recommended reading *Mere Christianity* by C. S. Lewis. It was difficult to understand and after reading only 20 pages, I gave up. I was so embarrassed; I didn't tell anyone but Bill. Then I poured over scripture, especially the New Testament, but I found myself asking more questions instead of finding answers. Knowledgeable of scripture and a man of faith, Bill couldn't help pull me through the darkness, though he tried. Why was I doubting? Why now? What would it take to make me believe?

Two weeks before my father's unexpected surgery, I asked Bill how I could brainwash myself to believe everything regarding the life and death of Jesus. He encouraged me to continue praying and reading scripture.

I so wanted to believe that Jesus, the perfect sacrifice, died on the cross for me and for all sinners. I wanted to totally embrace the fact that his resurrection meant he conquered death for all believers. I cried out to God, "I want to believe; please rid me of my doubts." I felt it would take a miracle to achieve this.

Little did I know at that time that I'd receive what I so needed. God would use my earthly father, the man who had always taught me so well, to be the vehicle by whom my faith would be restored. In the surgical waiting room, when I heard the words, "If I raised my Son from the dead, don't you think I can give you back your father?" I knew God was affirming the authenticity of scripture, His mercy, and His almighty power. With a wave of peace, He washed away the doubts that had plagued me for months.

Yes, I believe in miracles. The severity of the blockages in my father's coronary vessels should have prevented him from even making it to the operating room, but he did and lived to tell the tale. God's audible words gave me peace not just for the moment but also for a lifetime. How privileged I was to witness two miracles in just one day.

Lesson Learned:

Sometimes our most valuable lessons are taught *through* individuals, not by them. I was reminded that God can do anything, anywhere, any time. He is the author of creation, the mastermind of salvation through His Son, Jesus Christ, and the maker of miracles.

Dad on the Oahu shoreline

GIVE GENEROUSLY

Romans 12:8

"If a man's gift is encouraging, let him encourage, if it is contributing to the needs of others, let him give generously."

GIVE GENEROUSLY

If there is anyone who has lived by the motto, "It is better to give than to receive," it has been Dad. From as early as I can recall, I've borne witness to his generous nature.

Even in the smallest gestures, his giving nature was evident. For many years, I believed that Dad really liked chicken wings. Whenever Mom fixed a whole chicken for dinner, he always chose the wings. I never understood why anyone would opt for pieces of meat that were 90 per cent bone. Much later in life, I realized it wasn't about what he was receiving but what he was able to give away. By selecting the worst, he offered the best to his wife and children.

Dad also loved to bring home treats whenever possible. A sack of assorted dilly bars from the local Dairy Queen always brought a smile to every face at home. He let everyone choose a flavor from the bag, and he got whatever dilly wasn't selected. The lone dilly was usually lime green flavored, which none of us liked. Whenever and wherever a "choice" was to be made, he always put everyone ahead of himself.

Dad's generosity spilled over into every relationship he had. He always offered to pay the tab regardless of who he was with or how many were present. As an adult, I've chuckled watching individuals at gatherings, however small or large, wait to see if someone might offer to pick up the tab. It's rare these days to find someone like Dad.

His willingness to give has spanned generations. Whenever a grandchild or youngster was in need, be it financial or emotional, Dad came to the rescue. He didn't need a shirt with a large S on it. That letter was tattooed on his heart. It could have stood for Skip, which was the name everyone knew him by, but it branded him as a true Superhero. He supported each cause, fundraiser, and every child.

Praise and attention were never Dad's goals. Though he was not a wealthy man by earthly standards, he nonetheless gave without ever asking or expecting anything in return. He did whatever he could to help anyone in any way, and he did it joyfully.

Although Dad, by nature, put himself last, it was in doing so that he came to be first in the hearts of his family and all who knew him.

Lesson Learned:

It is my belief that generous parents often breed generous children. This is not because of an inherited gene, but rather a learned behavior. I was fortunate to have been raised by a man who gave generously in all aspects of his life. It is my hope to emulate this giving spirit both in my home and the outside world.

Skip's 6 grandchildren: Joshua, Maggie, Sam, Claire, Britteny, and Shannon (Thanksgiving 2000)

The entire Campbell Clan (Thanksgiving 2003)

NEVER SURRENDER TO THE ENEMY

2 Samuel 22:40

"You armed me with strength for battle; you made my adversaries bow at my feet."

NEVER SURRENDER TO THE ENEMY

There is an old Indian adage, "You can't know someone until you've walked a mile in his moccasins." Although there was a time in my life that I wished I could have swapped shoes with another, I would have never wanted anyone to experience the dark days and nights along this particular path.

Two months after having a medically recommended total hysterectomy, at the age of 44, I fell into a deep depression. Tears seemed to continually stream down my cheeks. I tried to hide my condition by retreating to my closet and covering myself with a blanket. It was frightening to not be in control. When I consulted my surgeon about my mental state, she simply said, "It's just going to take time."

Inevitably, my entire family realized that my post-op recovery had taken a major spiral downward into depths unknown to them. Hormonal changes within my body accounted for agonizing insomnia. Though I had tried several oral estrogen replacement medications, all of them caused severe migraine headaches and were discontinued. I so desperately wanted to sleep, but all I could do was lie down and weep.

Since I was unable to function in any role, my parents came to live at our home to help with Claire and Maggie and offer whatever assistance they could. Dad would sit next to me on our couch, hugging me to himself as my head rested on his chest. The sound of his heartbeat was the only "music" which soothed my soul long enough to enable me to drift off to sleep for, at most, 30 minutes.

Mom and Dad tried to encourage me, but I felt the situation to be hopeless. I think Dad feared that I would give up on life. He was determined not to let that happen. On multiple occasions, with help from Mom, he put my shoes on my feet and lifted me off the couch. He would half-carry me out our front door and literally drag me around our yard.

The crisp autumn air slapped my face with each step as he pleaded with me to keep trying. "You can't give up. Just keep putting one foot in front of the other," he repeated on every excursion. "You've got to keep fighting," he commanded. When I wanted to stop, he dragged me further. I have no doubt that this old staff sergeant would have carried me on his back if it meant keeping me alive during this war.

My condition did not improve, and I was admitted to a psychiatric ward on Halloween, four weeks after my depression began. I had lost 25 pounds in two months and seemed to be a shell of the person I had once been. I was not suicidal but had stated I didn't want to live in my current condition. I never thought I would leave the hospital alive. Although I had not enlisted for this conflict, I knew God was my commander-in-chief. I claimed His sovereignty as I accepted "my orders" each day. An antidepressant medication was started, and I was discharged five days after admission.

In follow-up, a female psychiatrist who was not involved with my case in the hospital and a female internist, who specializes in hormonal issues, recommended starting estrogen patch therapy and changing antidepressant medications. This drug combination, after several weeks, helped turn the tide of my battle with depression.

I would never have imagined that anything positive could result from such a frightening ordeal. Looking back, I now realize it was necessary for me to spend time in a foxhole so that I might have the empathy and knowledge to help others in the midst of combat. The experience also drew me closer to God and to every member of my family.

I will forever be grateful to my husband, mother, siblings, children, and friends for supporting me in the fight for and of my life. I will also never forget my father carrying me on the battlefield and comforting me in the trenches.

Lesson Learned:

No matter how dark the days or nights are, don't surrender to the enemy. Strength for the battle will come from family, friends, medical professionals, and God. Don't ever give up.

A verse which comforted me during the darkest days and nights of my life is 1 Peter 5:10:

"And the God of all grace, who called you to his eternal glory in Christ, after you have suffered for a little while, will himself restore you and make you strong, firm, and steadfast."

ENCOURAGE EACH OTHER

1 Thessalonians 5:11

"Therefore encourage one another and build each other up, just as in fact you are doing."

ENCOURAGE EACH OTHER

Although I was much improved four weeks after my hospitalization for depression, I still struggled with leading a "normal" life. It was early December and the thought of leaving my house, much less shopping for Christmas presents, frightened me. I was not confident in any public setting.

One morning, while talking to Dad on the phone, I sadly told him I doubted whether I would be able to prepare for the holidays. He told me not to be concerned with giving anyone a gift. "No one expects a thing, Lor," he said. "Someday, when you're feeling up to it, just write me a poem," he requested.

I had always loved writing poetry from the time I was a teen. The problem was that I felt my creativity had been lost after my depression and hospitalization. I wasn't sure I would ever be the person I was prior to the operation.

"I don't think I'll ever be able to do that," I told him. "I'm not sure I can write anymore."

"Lor, I know you have many more poems to write," he encouragingly stated. Not wanting to pressure me in any way, he added, "You don't have to do it now; just think of it as an I.O.U."

I hung up the phone, not giving a second thought to my father's request. Several days after the conversation, I suddenly felt an urge to write. Initially, I was nervous. I wasn't sure I would be able to follow through on my prompting. As I wrote line upon line, I felt as though a wall had come crashing down within me. For the first time since my surgery, I felt like the person I had always known myself to be. When I finished the following poem, I knew I had the perfect Christmas gift for my father.

Not Forsaken

I have been down a road traveled by few
> definitely not yellow, instead a dark blue.

Running at first with no need for sleep,
> I wasn't sure this pace I could keep.

Then gravel appeared and I fell to my knees
> unable to stand and unable to please.

A familiar voice told me to sit and to rest.
> We sat on the ground with my head on his chest.

His soothing heartbeat, his comforting arm,
> allowed me to rest and not think of harm.

Then with his strength he forced me to stand,
> shuffling further, being led by his hand.

So many days I struggled on the road,
> thankful for tiny hands which lessened my load.

Gentle hands I had known all of my life,
> never realizing their strength, until this strife.

Sideline encouragement let me know others were there.
> Sustenance came from their love and their prayer.

Weary and hopeless I was carried for a way.
> The rocky path was too much as I stumbled each day.

Crying out to the Lord, "Where have you been?"
> Then realizing ignorance was my greatest sin.

For the voice, hands, back, and sideline cheers
> Were all "Jesus with skin," conquering my fears.

A fork in the road let me choose another way,
> now I gingerly step on yellow each day.

I'm not searching for Oz or my divine call.
> I'm just counting my blessings once and for all.

By the end of December, I was able to comfortably leave my house and do the Christmas shopping. We joyfully celebrated Jesus' birth and my rebirth at my home that December 25.

I don't think anyone appreciated his gift as much as Dad. With tears in his eyes, he silently read the framed poem. Looking up at me, he simply said, "You done good, kid."

Dad and Mom reading "Not Forsaken" (Christmas 2002)

Of all the poems I've written, *Not Forsaken* means the most. It is evidence that my creativity did not die in my battle with depression. I think Dad knew I needed encouragement to prove to myself that I hadn't lost anything more than a uterus and two ovaries. His gift request was the best present *I received* that holiday season.

Lesson Learned:

Encouragement comes in many different forms. It can be verbal or written, subtle or obvious, and given in good or bad times. Regardless of its nature, encouragement is always appreciated. We should never hesitate to offer a kind word, a hug, or a suggestion to someone who is in need.

Dad knew I was struggling with many issues after my hospitalization. By encouraging me to write, he brought me one step closer to a full recovery. Dad had been correct. *Not Forsaken* was the first of many poems I would eventually write.

Claire, Maggie, Bill, and me (Christmas 2002)

LOVE UNCONDITIONALLY AND CONTINUALLY

2 Chronicles 20:21

"Give thanks to the Lord, for His love endures forever."

LOVE UNCONDITIONALLY AND CONTINUALLY

All of the preceding stories have a common thread. They all are evidence that my father loved me continually and unconditionally.

Simply put, my dad taught me what love *was* because he embodied what love *is*. Through his actions and words, I experienced the love as described by the Apostle Paul in 1 Corinthians 13:

"Love is patient, love is kind. It does not envy, it does not boast, it is not proud. It is not rude, it is not self-seeking, it is not easily angered, it keeps no record of wrongs. Love does not delight in evil, but rejoices in the truth. It always protects, always trusts, always hopes, always perseveres."

This kind of love goes against our natural tendencies. It is only by becoming more like Christ that we are able to love unselfishly, expecting nothing in return. Because I experienced this kind of love from my earthly father, it enabled me to understand and appreciate the love of my Heavenly Father. Even though I've made mistakes, Dad has never stopped loving me. He's walked with me, supported me, and at times, even carried me through trials and tribulations. This is what our Heavenly Father does as well.

God's love is constant, limitless, and everlasting. It is with us over our lifetime here on earth, and beyond. It is with us through every peak and valley we encounter along life's journey. This is verified in scripture.

Paul teaches us in Ephesians 3:17-19:

"And I pray that you, being rooted and established in love, may have power, together with all the saints, to grasp how wide and long and high and deep is the love of Christ, and to know this love that surpasses all knowledge…"

In Romans 8:38-39, we are told "that neither death nor life, neither angels nor demons, neither the present nor the future, nor any powers, neither height nor depth, nor anything else in all creation, will be able to separate us from the love of God that is in Christ Jesus, our Lord."

Lesson Learned:

I'll forever be grateful to my earthly father for loving me so dearly that I could understand and know the love of my Heavenly Father. Dad's lessons gave me roots which rest firmly embedded in the soil of his love. I believe there is no greater love than evidenced by our Heavenly Father allowing His Son to take on the sin of the world and be sacrificed, offering salvation to all sinners. His Word provides a written record of history, wisdom, and instruction for our lives.

Romans 15:4 tells us, "For everything that was written in the past was written to teach us, so that through the endurance taught in the Scriptures and the encouragement they provide we might have hope."

As stated in John 15:17, we have been appointed to go and bear fruit---**fruit that will last.** It is my hope to bear "good fruit," bringing glory to God and giving testimony to having been nurtured, here on earth, by one of the best.

Dad and me celebrating his 77th birthday (2-12-09)

TRUST IN THE LORD

Proverbs 3:5

"Trust in the Lord with all your heart and lean
not on your own understanding."

TRUST IN THE LORD

Little did I know that this final chapter would be written after my book had been edited. What seemed like a completed work was not. Dad still needed to teach me one more lesson.

The sun was shining, and it was a beautiful day in June, as I drove to Mom and Dad's home to accompany Dad to his scheduled cardiac stress test. During the hour and a half drive, I daydreamed of the fun-filled days ahead. My daughter, Maggie, was home from college, and I knew the house would be filled with activity and laughter. I was also anxious to begin the laborious task of fine-tuning my writing.

I arrived hours before the appointment. Dad and I played our favorite game of "show and tell." I showed him six old fishing baits I purchased at a recent yard sale, and he told me their approximate worth. Then, he showed me his latest thrift sale acquisitions: a solid brass mortar and pestle and a clarinet. Though he did not play the clarinet, he couldn't pass up buying this beautiful black instrument stored neatly in its pristine case. Just for fun, he joked he might teach himself how to play it.

We said a quick good-bye to Mom, reassuring her we'd be back in a couple of hours, and left for the hospital. While I drove, Dad spoke with my eldest daughter, Claire, on my cell phone during a break in her graduate studies. Their conversation centered on Claire's ragdoll kitten. Dad jokingly advised her to name it, "Oh boy." As usual, the conversation ended with him commenting that she would someday win a Nobel Prize.

As we entered the hospital, Dad turned to me and said, "I'm not going to be able to go very far on the treadmill." I responded, "Just walk as far as you can, and stop whenever you have to."

I patiently waited in the hallway, talking to other patients while my father began the stress test. Within minutes, my father's cardiologist entered the room that Dad was in. I rose and followed him as he entered.

Dad had collapsed on the treadmill after only 90 seconds. He was lying down, but talking as I approached. He appeared relieved that there was evidence for his lack of energy over the past several months. As two intravenous (IV) lines were started, he looked at me and said, "I knew I wasn't going to do well."

An emergency cardiac catheterization was ordered. I asked the staff to place a urinary catheter as Dad would be lying flat for hours after the procedure. As he was wheeled away he asked that Mom not be called. "We don't want to have her worry any sooner than she has to," he said.

Dad always protected Mom--it was his nature. I disobeyed him for the first time in my adult life as I phoned Mom. I knew that Dad would probably need surgery, and I wanted her to know what was happening and what I thought would happen.

Results revealed my dad's aortic valve was in worse condition than previously thought. He also had serious blockage in three of his old bypass grafts. Surgery was recommended and scheduled for the next day.

Dad was admitted to the Critical Care Unit (CCU). His nurse appeared overwhelmed and stated that "it" was hectic. I mentioned that Dad hadn't received any of his daily medications since he had been instructed not to take any prior to the stress test. Since he had two IVs running and had been given two dosages of IV dye, I was most concerned that he receive Lasix, his water pill. He had a history of congestive heart failure and had been treated in the emergency room months earlier for fluid accumulation in his lungs. Since his aortic valve was in worse condition than what had been thought, his fluid balance was crucial. The nurse's response was simply, "I haven't been able to even get my hands on his chart because so many people want it." She then left his room.

Dad repetitively tried to clear his throat. He said it felt as though something was stuck in his chest. The nurse reappeared, and I asked if I could give Dad his Lasix. He had brought all of his medications from home to the hospital. "No," she said. "We don't want patients taking any medication from home once they've been admitted to the hospital."

My father had developed rales (crackles) which could be heard when he opened his mouth and took a breath. This is a sign fluid is building up in the lungs. It was a sign that both Mom and Dad knew well since Dad had experienced it in the past.

Dad and I thought help was on the way when a young male physician's assistant (PA) entered the room to do a physical.

"How are you doing, sir?" he asked my father.

"Well, I'm a little nervous. You see I normally take Lasix, and I haven't had any yet today. Listen…" Dad then opened his mouth for the PA to hear the audible crackles. I was shocked that the PA didn't seem concerned. Had I been out of medicine so long that what I perceived to be a concerning sign was in fact not? The PA left the room without addressing our concern.

Shortly after my mom and sister arrived, Dad's nurse re-entered the room. I requested the Lasix again. Dad had already shown Mom how bad the crackles were. He was coughing intermittently as he tried to eat a meal, which had been sitting out for some time. I was angry. I had tried not to throw my professional weight around--I had been polite. Now, hours after he had been admitted, I stated in front of family members, "If she doesn't bring the Lasix in the next 15 minutes, I'll run down the hall screaming like Shirley McClaine in the movie, *Terms of Endearment.*"

That scene re-enactment did not need to take place as the nurse finally appeared 10 minutes later saying she had the Lasix. Before it was given, my sister, Jill, suggested we leave the room to give Mom and Dad time to talk before the surgery. We decided to get Mom a take-out meal, as she had not eaten dinner. By the time we returned, Mom had been asked to sit in the family lounge as Dad was having difficulty breathing. She had been told he had pulmonary edema.

I quickly entered his room. He was seated in a chair and seemed relieved to see my face. An assisted breathing machine was in place.

He lifted his breathing mask and said, "Lor, the oral Lasix isn't strong enough. I need IV Lasix." Trying not to show my fear or anger, I cringed. The nurse had given him oral Lasix--it had not been given intravenously as I had assumed it would be, due to all the clinical signs indicating fluid overload.

When Lasix was finally administered intravenously, Dad was on a roller coaster, headed only in one direction--down. The on-call cardiologist decided Dad should be intubated. An aortic balloon pump was placed, and surgery was scheduled for early morning.

I tried to sleep in a small conference room adjacent to the family lounge. I prayed fervently for a miracle. I cried out to the Lord. I felt God was telling me that He is Jehovah Jireh and the God of miracles.

Not remembering what Jehovah Jireh meant, I quickly looked it up on the hospital's computer before Dad was taken to the operating room. It means "God will provide." I assumed God would provide a miraculous healing despite discovering there was lab evidence indicating Dad had suffered a heart attack at some point after admission. Dad was in critical condition going into surgery.

I waited with family in the crowded lounge. Hour after hour passed as we sat, trying to comfort Mom and each other. We rejoiced when we finally heard that Dad had survived the day-long surgery.

The surgeon came to the lounge and told us that Dad was a very sick man and had a fifty/fifty chance. I became disheartened when he informed us that Dad's chest would be left open. I had never witnessed a cardiac patient coming out of surgery without chest closure and took this as a very negative sign.

I left the hospital and sat in my parked van. I called a dear friend and asked for her prayers. I knew she would ask others to do the same. Jill came to the van and escorted me to the hospital's chapel. I wept as I read 2 Kings 20:5-6 aloud. In it, King Hezekiah is told by Isaiah that the Lord heard his prayer, saw his tears, and healed him. The Lord added 15 years to Hezekiah's life. Since I had walked through Hezekiah's tunnel in Israel, his life story was very real to me. I felt strength in praying scripture. I returned to the family lounge after Claire, who had driven over 300 miles to reach the hospital, came to the chapel to give me an update. She informed me that Dad's status had improved and the decision was made to close his chest in the operating room.

Within hours of Dad's surgery, he coded in the CCU. I instinctively threw off my jacket and ran to his bedside. I stood at the foot of the bed, out of the way, and shouted, "Fight, Dad, fight!" Within a short period of time his vital signs stabilized. In my life, I've run to numerous codes, mostly when I was a pediatric intern, but this was the first time I prayed throughout the code. I awaited the miracle of Dad's healing, which I was certain would take place.

Dad coded several more times over the course of the night and following morning. In an attempt to remove a small clot near his heart, an emergency thoracotomy (surgical opening of the chest) was performed in the CCU. When family was finally allowed to enter his room, Mom asked me to accompany her to his bedside. I took her small hand as we gingerly stepped into his room. The nurse greeted us by saying, "We can't do CPR any longer because his chest is open. We can only maintain him with drugs."

After hearing that sentence and looking at my father's swollen discolored face, Mom said, "Lor, we've got to let him go." I never questioned this courageous statement--I was in full agreement. Mom wanted the madness to end. She could not bear to have her beloved husband suffer any longer. I believe the nurse and PA were relieved that Mom made this decision since Dad's death was imminent.

Holding Mom's hand and supporting her weight, we approached the lounge where multiple family members and friends had gathered; some had traveled hundreds of miles to offer prayers and support. I told them of Mom's decision. It was also her request that no one enter Dad's room. She did not want anyone to be traumatized by his distorted appearance.

I retreated with Mom and Bill to the small conference room I had tried to sleep in the previous night. I shook uncontrollably and couldn't speak a complete sentence without stuttering. Mom, distraught over my breakdown, left the room.

Moments later Claire appeared and knelt before me. "Mom, I know you're not doing well, but please don't let Grandpa die alone.

You're the only one who can go in. Grandma doesn't want any of us to see him."

I immediately rose, tears streaming down my face and stumbled to Dad's room, with Bill following. Shaking and trembling, I sat in a chair massaging one of the few areas without an intravenous line--his right foot. Having previously entered despite Mom's concerns, Jill stood near the head of the bed. I rose to speak in Dad's ear one final time. I apologized for letting him down and told him how much he meant to me--how much he had always meant to me. Holding his hand as best I could, I promised him that I would care for Mom until they were together again. A few short minutes after I spoke my last words to Dad, he passed from this life to the next at 12:34 PM.

After all of the tubes and lines were removed, family members were allowed to spend time with him. Bill and I were the last to leave. I don't remember ever calling my father, Daddy, but now, I could not stop repeating, "Oh, Daddy," as I lay across his covered, open chest. I didn't want to leave him--ever. "I just can't leave him," I said as I looked at Bill, tears streaming down my face. I stomped my foot and wanted to scream. I wanted to run away with Dad fastened to my back. I didn't want to leave my teacher… my father…my friend. I stood sobbing uncontrollably. Bill tenderly embraced me as he whispered--"Lor, it's time to go." I left and didn't look back. I knew if I did that I would run back to Dad.

For 72 hours, I agonized, reliving every moment from talking about fishing baits to his last words before intubation. I was flooded with guilt. I had always tried to protect my mom and dad in every health care situation. How could I have failed my father so miserably? He always introduced me as his personal physician. Why didn't I scream for the Lasix hours before it was given? Why did I leave his bedside? Why didn't the nurse or PA act on our requests? How could God allow Dad to die after he had survived the day-long surgery? Why… Why…Why? I wanted to curl up and have someone hide me away until I died.

As I lay in despair, I suddenly wondered what Dad would say to me. Without even thinking, I knew. I had nearly 51 years of lessons to draw from.

It's water under the bridge, Lor.

You're not worth a tinker's damn if you stay like this.

If you can do something to prevent this from happening to some other poor guy, do it.

I knew he was right. Dad would want me to go on. He had always forgiven me, motivated me, and encouraged me. I needed to honor him and all of the lessons he had taught me over the years.

So, where was my heavenly Father in all of this? God had reminded me that He is Jehovah Jireh and the God of miracles…so what happened?

While waiting to see my father after the thoracotomy, I remembered an event that occurred during my trip to Israel. We had visited the Upper Room, the place where the Last Supper and Pentecost are thought to have occurred. While listening to beautiful music in this room, I suddenly became nauseous. Sweaty and hot, I looked for an exit, but the crowds prevented me from leaving. I turned to dear friends and told them I felt ill. They immediately began praying for me and within minutes I felt a release. The nausea left as I began to cry. I heard God say to me, "Lori, I understand how much you love your earthly father, but, you need to--you must-- put your full trust and heart in me, your Heavenly Father." These are the words as recorded in my journal. For over a year, God had been preparing me for this moment.

I had to trust God. I felt that I always had, but this was a time when my trust was being tested. I needed to rest, knowing that Jehovah Jireh would provide the strength and grace for me and my family to go on. I know God can perform miracles, but He chose not to perform the miracle I was expecting. Though I cannot understand that decision, I will trust God who sees eternally backward and eternally forward. He knows all, sees all, and understands all. His ways are not our ways. He is sovereign. What we want may not be what is best for us or the world.

Grief can lead to despair and hopelessness. It is only by truly trusting God, regardless of our situation, that peace, which passes all human understanding, can be experienced.

Dad's death brought me to the edge of the cliff where you either jump into the arms of Jesus or fall to the depths alone. With tears in my eyes and a giant hole in my chest, I am raising both hands in praise to an ever-faithful, all-knowing God, whom I trust. Resting in the arms of my savior, I will go on teaching His lessons and my dad's, until the day I can embrace them both.

Lesson Learned:

We cannot hold on to our earthly fathers though many of us wish we could. As believers in our Lord, Jesus Christ, we are assured of a reunion with fellow believers that will last for eternity. True peace comes only from trusting God, regardless of situation or circumstance.

"Find rest, O my soul, in God alone; my hope comes from Him. He alone is my rock and my salvation; He is my fortress, I will not be shaken. My salvation and my honor depend on God; He is my mighty rock, my refuge. Trust in him at all times, O people; pour out your hearts to Him, for God is our refuge." Psalm 62: 5-8

God so graciously met me on the shore in Galilee and again in the Upper Room, not only to prepare me for the loss of my father, but to be a vessel by which His words could be shared…"Fear Not… I AM." I can trust Him and so can you.

"And in the end, it's not the years in your life that count.

It's the life in your years."

-Abraham Lincoln

EPILOGUE

One of the most difficult things I've done in my life was writing my father's obituary. One can't capture the essence of a life in a few paragraphs. For that reason, I am grateful for this book. Given to my father as a Christmas present in 2008, it now serves as a tribute to him.

Dad receiving "Lessons Learned From My Father" (Christmas 2008)

After Dad's death, my mother received numerous cards and letters from his previous students. Some of these individuals were students in the first high school class my father taught, over 50 years ago. All condolences that we received cited my father as the best teacher they had known. It is evident that Dad had an impact regardless of who, what, or where he taught.

As we've sorted through various boxes in my parents' house and garage, I have found various agates scattered throughout their contents. I like to think Dad placed them there, just for me.

Bill graciously took me agate hunting on two separate occasions in the weeks following Dad's death. Though I cried as I walked the north shore of Lake Superior and in the gravel pits south of our home, I felt comforted. I feel closest to Dad searching for the rocks he taught me to find.

The old fishing baits I showed Dad, before his cardiac stress test, are now displayed in my home. Pictures of him at various ages stand next to these old lures. I plan to teach any future grandchildren to bait their hooks in hopes of catching a "big one," and tell them how Jesus can help us all to be fishers of men.

Although my family and I miss my father terribly, we know he would want us to stay strong, have fun, and continue being role models for future generations.

It is my sincerest hope to effectively model the lessons taught to me. I pray my writing brings honor to my dad and glory to my Heavenly Father.

May those who read this book feel not just the love of a man, but the love of their Creator as well.

One Stone

Tossed into the water,
    one solitary stone.
Not aware of its effect,
    having been alone.
One ripple, then another,
    all expanding out.
Each affecting what's to come,
    of that there is no doubt.
Abruptly, the stone then rests,
    out of sight...in the dark.
But its impact is for all to see,
    for it has left a mark.

(Lori Campbell 2009)

Torches lit in honor of Dad at eldest granddaughter's wedding (10-3-09)

ACKNOWLEDGMENTS

First and foremost, I thank my dad for always encouraging me to write. Dad's response after reading the collection of stories in December 2008 was, "Lor, you only wrote about the good times." I responded, "That's all I remember." Dad was not one who sought to be in the spotlight. I know he felt that I had made him out to look like a saint. In my eyes, Dad was one. He will forever remain the wind beneath my wings. His lessons are a constant reminder of what true faith is about.

"Do not merely listen to the word, and so deceive yourselves. Do what it says. Anyone who listens to the word but does not do what it says is like a man who looks at his face in a mirror and, after looking at himself, goes away and immediately forgets what he looks like. But the man who looks intently into the perfect law that gives freedom, and continues to do this, not forgetting what he has heard, but doing it---he will be blessed in what he does." James 1:22-25

Thank you Bill, Claire, and Maggie for the emotional support I needed to complete this project during a year filled with grief and change. Thanks, too, for all of the hours each of you spent proofing my work. Your love keeps me going and writing.

This book would have never become a reality without my editor, Beth Erickson. Thank you, Beth, for all of the time and effort spent on making this project the best it could be. I will always believe our meeting was not by chance, but God-directed. God bless you.

A special thank you to Wendy Rabe, who worked on the original layout and format of the book. Your patience and time were so very appreciated.

To friends Jay, Jane, and Ruth, thank you for your encouragement throughout this entire process. Your kind words and prayers continue to sustain me.

I am so grateful to Dennis O'Hara of Northern Images Photography. Thank you for allowing the use of your beautiful agate photographs in the design of the book cover.

Claire…how do I say thank you with mere words? You knew when to step in and lead me across the finish line. I will forever be grateful for your knowledge, assistance, and love.

Praise be to my Heavenly Father for giving me the inspiration to write my stories in conjunction with His Word. It is my hope that my written words might lift spirits, re-direct lives, and bring individuals closer to knowing and feeling the love of God. To God be the glory!

"You held onto my hand for almost 51 years...you will hold onto my heart forever. Love you, Dad."

-Lori

"May the God of hope fill you with all joy and peace as you trust in him, so that you may overflow with hope by the power of the Holy Spirit."

Romans 15:13

www.ingramcontent.com/pod-product-compliance
Lightning Source LLC
Chambersburg PA
CBHW081511040426

42447CB00013B/3183